BHARAT IN TONES ANEW

THE MODI UPSWING AND PAST REGIMES

BHARAT IN TONES ANEW

THE MODI UPSWING AND PAST REGIMES

Anand Swaroop Kashiv

Foreword by

General (Dr) Vijay Kumar Singh (Retd)
PVSM, AVSM, YSM

PENTAGON PRESS LLP

First published in 2025 by
PENTAGON PRESS LLP
206, Peacock Lane, Shahpur Jat
New Delhi-110049, India
Contact: 011-26490600

Typeset in Times New Roman, 11.5 Point
Printed by Aegean Offset Printers, Greater Noida, U.P.

ISBN 978-81-968722-3-6 (HB)

Disclaimer: The views and opinions expressed in the book is the individual assertion of the Author. The Publisher does not take any responsibility for the same in any manner whatsoever. The same shall solely be the responsibility of the Author.

www.pentagonpress.in

*"To my son Kedaar,
who continue to inspire me
to tell stories that matter"*

Contents

जनरल (डा.) विजय कुमार सिंह
पीवीएसएम, एवीएसएम, वाईएसएम (से.नि.)

GEN (DR) VIJAY KUMAR SINGH
PVSM, AVSM, YSM (Retd)

राज्य मंत्री
सड़क परिवहन, राजमार्ग;
एवं नागर विमानन मंत्रालय
भारत सरकार

Minister of State for
Road Transport, Highways
and Civil Aviation
Government of India

FOREWORD

An academic work emanating from the pen of an activist and social reformer needs to be welcomed as a surprise package. The author deserves to be congratulated as he emerges from the world of real time politics and social service. He has attempted a very wide canvas ranging from the tenor and the founding tale of foreign policy and Diplomacy since the Nehruvian times all the way to the robust and effective narrative pursued during the present time. This span is not easy but Anand attains it with precision. The Book declares with aplomb the differences and consonance of the Modi's times with other leaders like Indira Gandhi, Rajeev Gandhi and Atal Bihari Vajpayee. The term Global South has been a much contested realm in International relations in the contemporary context and finds a mention as such. The author asserts that the Indian foreign policy strain in the times of Nehruvian idealism stressed for strategic autonomy by not entering into the fences of cold war rivalry.

Similarly, PM Modi has also managed the playing out of a balancing act between Russia, USA and many more contesting nations. Author asserts that under Modi's challenging Global landscape, India has been able to be more aggressive, proactive and has adopted a muscular approach to foreign policy intent and Diplomatic intent. The stress has been on the larger than life avatar of Vishwaguru delineated by the constraints of Pragmatic and Realist foreign policy formulations.

International Relations are a discipline that can be deciphered through the multiple prisms of National interest, Diplomacy and Foreign Policy. The work posits the stable and status quoist and regressive overtures of the Nehruvian international relations and foreign policy.

Indian external firmament was exposed to the ideas of cold war and the skulduggery of the intertwined rivalry of Great powers and the manner in which the nation veered post 1947. The masthead of the movement of Non alignment and decolonization placed the Indian image and role on a higher moral pedestal. The author brings out pithily and bluntly that India marched ahead in the post-independence period with a rather too Idealist mantle towards the challenges the world threw at India.

It was assumed that India was a socialist nation which drew the nation away from the NATO block of countries. The author expresses the sentiment that the distrust and suspicion towards United States framed a self-defeating strain of Foreign policy plank for Bharat. This is an academic risk that the author confidently takes in order to drive home his point of view, opinion and perception that he is prejudiced and biased towards the Nehruvian policy myth of the nation in a post-colonial phase of Bharat. The author painstakingly points at the principles of Indira Gandhi's Foreign Policy which was an avowed success and brought great military success leading to the birth of Bangladesh. The author here clinically depoliticizes himself and heaps praise for the robust networking and foreign policy of Indira Gandhi. He dabbles briefly with the Chinese overtures of Rajeev Gandhi and appreciates his risk taking and innovative thinking vis a vis China. He draws out a detailed sketch of Indian bilateral trysts between New Delhi and Washington as also India's friendship with Soviet Union. In Modi ji's time, the India-US relationship has progressed and prospered in a boundless manner with only the Indo-US nuclear deal being a precedent to the relationship. The relationship is now dubbed as a 'Strategic Partnership' and a 'Defence Alliance' between India and the United States of America. Prime Minister Narendra Modi spoke to the American population and the Indian Diaspora which had travelled far-off distances from across the length and expanse of the United States of America. The author very evocatively contends that Prime Minister Narendra Modi spoke about relations with USA as also elaborated and extolled upon India's progress.

Human security is the order of the day in the larger International System. In a world beset by war and aggressive politics, peace and developmental concerns are hampered and obstructed. Author highlights the negotiation ethics of G20 as a platform of diplomacy, wherein, the concerns of the South or the developmental needs of the developing nations assume prominent global concern. This is not merely paying lip service to the decisions and monopoly of the First World and developed comity of nations. One point of focus can be the global commons of food security, climate change action, gender empowerment, poverty eradication and conflict resolution which are pertinent requirements of a besieged international system. Author points out that the hiatus between the rising developing world and the First World can be emphatically seen. Emphasis is on the idiom of human security, development and growth that the author brings out

Refreshingly. Modian consensus posits India at the cusp of the much talked about Amrit Kal in the larger International System. The proactive and the aggressive foreign policy has received multifarious reviews but this one by Anand is a special and evocative one as the comparisons with the past denominations and places the work in a completely different realm where brave criticism of Nehru becomes the founding drive of the academic work.

(General (Dr) V.K. Singh (Retd))

Preamble: The Introduction to the Narrative

International Relations is a new subject and quite a contemporary academic discipline going by what avid observers or scholars of the subject claim. One cannot deny the fact that international relations or world politics reflects the trends in the knowledge pantheon in the West and the United States of America. IR, as the succinct and short form goes, pertains to relations between nation-states and their citizens, that is, the commoners in all imaginable spheres of societal, political, economic and cultural domains of international affairs. In the contemporary times of New Delhi's external affairs dimensions, India's foreign policy is assuming a shift to super power status wherein India is already being accorded the status of a Great Power which aims to develop into a developed nation by the end of the Amrit Kal period by 2047.

The first academic chair to teach and accumulate knowledge in the sphere of International Relations was established in the University of Abrswyth in the USA. Since long, IR has been construed as the last neglected chapter in political science or political theory. The task for a researcher or an academician of IR is to undertake a mainstreaming and bring into the relevance of the discipline separately other than the wider and much broader ambit of political studies or political science.

The possibility of an 'Indian' conception of international affairs presents a vexed, and often highly politicised debate. Unsurprisingly, the discussion is often framed in terms of India's 'rising' status, mirroring developments in China and elsewhere. It raises deeper questions over the autonomy and purpose of the social sciences as a whole. Indeed, the quest for an 'Indian' contribution to international relations (IR) foregrounds a wider debate now taking place in the discipline over the need for a 'global IR'.

Similar to the notion that the bureaucracy is known as the steel framework of the nation's governance mechanisms and public administration, the Indian Foreign Service does an immense exercise of forging a positive, regal and royal image of India in order to facilitate trade. When IFS officers complete their probations, they are designated as consuls and first and second officers of the embassy they are sent to. It involves a lot of event management and the amplificatory implementation of India's national interests. Still, one fact needs to be remembered that opposite to the Chinese diplomacy and the expanse of its Confucian centres all across the length and breadth of the global polity, the numbers and the numerical strength and not their skills are considered to be inadequate for the propagation of the name and fame of Bharat.

The luxury of external postings ranging from the tropics of Brazil to the urban finesse of Tokyo and Washington earns our Foreign Service the ire and jealousy of the other services. Thus, the organization of the Indian Foreign Service and their training at the prestigious Foreign Service institutes prepares them for a hard working but luxurious and posh career ahead in the heady portals of the embassies or the MEA based in New Delhi, Mumbai and Kolkata.

In the Ministry of External Affairs, the Foreign Secretary, in consultation with the various joint secretaries and the External Affairs Minister forms the deciding team or the decision-making outfit for the country. The web portal of the Ministry of External Affairs informs us that "The origin of the Indian Foreign Service can be traced back to British rule when the Foreign Department was created to conduct business with the 'Foreign European Powers'. In fact, it was on 13 September 1783 that the Board of Directors of the East India Company passed a resolution at Fort William, Calcutta (now Kolkata), to create a department that could help "relieve the pressure" on the Warren Hastings administration. He conducted its "secret and political business".

Subsequently known as the 'Indian Foreign Department', it went ahead with the expansion of diplomatic representation, wherever necessary, to protect British interests."

India's Foreign policy has witnessed a chequered existence wherein the larger context of national interest and diplomacy emerges as a trite nomenclature which can be interchangeably utilised. India has a mythological background and through the tenets of the Sanatana Dharma been the birthplace of Lord Rama which literally means, 'To Ram' or 'to be happy content and just' in the routine rituals of one's self akin to a sage of Bharatvarsha. Along with it, it can be contended that the imagination of the concept of Rashtra came much before the understanding and comprehension of the larger tenet of the idiom of a nation–state. This was postulated by the historical treaty of Westphalia and the battle of Osnabruck in 1648.

When we refer to the word 'Preamble' are in fact adhering to and positing our comprehension of the national civilization that Bharatvarsha is. We are not adhering to the words of a 'Socialist, Secular Republic' but in multiple ways are talking about the foundational myth of Bharat. The historical and cultural moorings of the nation, that is Bharat, hark back to the panoply of Neolithic years when the understanding of a national collectivism was still finding its roots in the ancient historical tradition of the land.

Thus, the inception of the notion of, Rashtra, is the substratum upon which the entire edifice of the nation is perched. We are not talking about regional and provincial satrapism but are adhering to the idiom that a healthy and stable welfarist socio-economic and cultural loop is the fountainhead of the dominion of national interest. One such foreign policy strengthening act can be a revalidation of the icons and freedom fighters of the nation.

Foreign policy is the act or a string of pearls linkage through which a nation forges treaties, agreements and cooperative mechanisms seeking peace and cordiality of cooperation with the immediate neighbourhood and the larger context of the international system. The nation forges new bonds and severs libel of discord from nations such, as, the Islamic

Republic of Pakistan and the People's Republic of China in order to survive and progress in a volatile and fast mutating international system. One can surmise that despite the core foreign policy streak in the nation being ushering in peace, non-volatility and camaraderie in the larger world, the notion of can the Indian nation act as a true blue leader in the global firmament. The stress is on the factoid that the *moksha* providing terminology of India being the Vishwaguru thus refurbishing Bharat as a global actor, is steeped in the nom de plume of peace and Vasudeva Kutumbakum.

Thus, foreign policy strengthened internally by the domesticity of stability and *Sarva Dharma Sambhav* can become the order of the day. A revalidation of the past freedom fighters for whom paeans have not been sung adequately can become the order of the day for the present-day rise of Bharat. The governmental stress upon the larger idiom of celebrating and re-enlivening the past through the heroes of our freedom fighting days, is a deft exercise in marketing. It sells the wares of the nation in the larger global firmament through which investments and global decision-making along with an enhanced role in the international organizations.

Acknowledgements

I am deeply indebted to General V.K Singh for their invaluable guidance, unwavering support, and profound insights throughout the journey of writing this book. Their expertise in the field of international relations and foreign policy has been instrumental in shaping my understanding and analysis. I am grateful for their encouragement and constructive feedback, which significantly enriched the quality of this work.

I am also deeply grateful to my wife Akanksha Pare Kashiv for her unwavering support, encouragement, and understanding during this endeavor. Her patience and belief in me have been instrumental in completing this project.

I would also like to express my gratitude to Dr. Shivshakti Nath Bakshi, Prof. Amit Sharma, Subhash Dabas, Dr. Sushil Pare, Dr. Manan Dwivedi, Bibhuti Bhushan, Rajat Sharma, Jayvardhan Joshi whose assistance and encouragement were indispensable in completing this project.

Thank you for your indispensable contributions.

Chapter One

The Idiom of Human Security

Human security is the order of the day in the larger international system. In a world beset by war and aggressive politics, peace and developmental concerns are hampered and obstructed. The notion highlights the negotiation ethics of G20 as a platform of diplomacy wherein the concerns of the South or the developmental needs of the developing nations assume prominent global concern. There is no n to merely pay lip service to the decisions and monopoly of the First World and developed comity of nations. One point of focus can be the global commons of food security, climate change action, gender empowerment, poverty eradication and conflict resolution which are pertinent requirements of a besieged international system with a Third. It should be realized that the hiatus between the rising developing world and the First World can be emphatically seen.

We can further latch on to the fact that after Indonesia, New Delhi now assumes the presidency of the G20. India assumes a global responsibility as a global regulator and a Third World leader. India is playing a key role in conflict resolution and other developmental and human security concerns in the developing and underdeveloped world. Regime formation becomes the order of the day, wherein myriad nations and their establishments strive to coalesce into a global whole. India's presidency of the G20 is a step in the right direction. India has been knocking for long at the threshold of becoming a great power status in which Indian leadership of a new reformed Global South can benchmark the arrival of a new power. A related development is that the Global South now does not believe in mere protestations against the North and the First World but aims to work as equal partners with the richness and expediency of a smart group of nations like never before. And, it is New Delhi which can make the Global South forge a new bridge between the contesting national interests and characters of the northern and southern countries. It will be a thaw between the Global North and South.

What is Human Security?

India has always been an initiator as far as the notion of human security globally is concerned with special emphasis on the Third World. The religious adherence to the theme of Sustainable Development Goals has been one of the foreign policy strengths of a nation on the upswing. Targets of precedence in poverty eradication, women empowerment, labour discourse and others add feathers in the cap of international organizations. These objectives are the ones which New Delhi, too has been striving for in the larger context of sustainability and returning to Mother Nature in the context of what we have usurped from her. In the earlier United Nations General Assembly gatherings too, PM Narendra Modi has assiduously raised the stand of India in the hallowed corridors of international peace and justice. He initiated the LiFE initiative in the august presence of United Nations Secretary-General Antonio Guiterres with the objective to attain a global green scenario.

It has been estimated by experts that even if one billion people of the global population of eight billion take up the onerous task of adopting a climate friendly and green lifestyle, there would be a drastic cutback by 20 per cent in the total carbon emissions of the larger international system. The LiFE mission was officially introduced at the Glasgow session of COP 26 in 2021. It was, in his words, "an international movement towards mindful and deliberate utilization, instead of mindless and destructive consumption" to bring the global system to a greener and much more sustainable future. It is here that the Santana perspective of human security goes back to the neophyte times of yesteryears. The National Security Strategy of the United States of America as expostulated by President Joe Biden too mentions India as being the epicentre of liberal democracy. The time is now ripe for India to take up a global leadership role along with the regulating role of the USA and other democratic denominations in the larger world.

The G20 conference of nations was initially defined as primarily an economic grouping. Since the turbulence and transformation in the geo-economics of the globe, a larger and much more eclectic perspective has been adhered to by New Delhi at the crucial Bali conference. Also significant was the Indian insistence on a no-war pact between the global comity of nations other than the impact of the pandemic and the Ukraine conflict and the resultant penury in food and energy supply chains. Despite being an economic construct, it encompasses elements ranging from block chain, global health architecture and emerging technologies to climate change, digital transformation and migration. Equity and inclusion are the other prominent concerns of the Bali Declaration with India assuming the leadership in the G20 till 2023.

The Brogen Project informs us, "In many countries, when people hear the phrase 'third world country', visions of impoverished countries struggling to meet basic human needs are the first to pop up. This might be true in today's society, but the original definition of a third world country referred to nations that lacked an alliance with either the USA or the former Soviet Union. In recent years, the term has come to define countries that have high poverty rates, economic instability and lack basic human necessities like access to water, shelter and food for its citizens. These countries are often underdeveloped, and in addition to widespread poverty, also have high mortality rates."[1] Thus, the disadvantaged sections of countries are placed under the nomenclature of the Third World. The low infant mortality rates along with scourges like illiteracy, widespread poverty and food insecurity along with malnutrition stand as some indicators of the notion of underachievement in the sphere of human security. Thus, we can conveniently posit the conceptual sect of a Third World. This slew of objectives sets Bharat's credo in the larger international firmament as a generous, humanitarian and philanthropic juggernaut on the rise which entails a peaceful rise of

New Delhi. The 'Rise' of nations such as China through a shroud of hidden aims which are concealed in the narrative of humane liberalism and crony capital, militate against the cooperative oeuvre in the Chinese foreign policy, if there is any.

In the context of the central thrust of India's foreign policy, New Delhi has always maintained that Kashmir is an integral part and parcel of the Bharatiya ethos. The nation is not prepared to compromise on its foundational edifice of territorial integrity and centrality of its narrative of nationhood. *The Statesman* reports that, "The Regime is proud of unveiling the Jammu and Kashmir Reorganization and Reservation Act's amendments, wherein the Government showcases that since the abrogation of Article 370, the entire state of Jammu and Kashmir has witnessed a fall in terror incidents in the beleaguered Valley to an appreciable 70 per cent. There has been no incident of stone pelting since 2022 and along with these positive developments, there have been only 48 incidents of infiltration along with two incidents of ceasefire violations."[2]

NOTES

1. Simone Williams, URL: https://borgenproject.org/definition-of-a-third-world-country/ (Online: Web), accessed on 1 October 2023.
2. Correspondent, 'Amit Shah discusses J and K,' *The Statesman*, 7 December 2023.

Chapter Two

Determinants of India's Foreign Policy

Ideally, the manner in which a nation manifests its domestic tensile strength and internal efficacy is through its foreign policy and diplomacy. The territory of the nation, the indelible sway of sovereignty, along with boundaries and the residing hoi polloi in the national land terrain form the traditional and classic yardsticks for a land and its people. This tenet qualifies Bharat, as a nation state in the strictly Westphalian notion of nationhood.

Ernest Renan defines a nation as an entity based on the free will of individuals forming a collective identity: "A nation is a soul, a spiritual principle. Two things, which in truth are but one, constitute this soul or spiritual principle. One lies in the past, one in the present. One is the possession in common of a rich legacy of memories; the other is present-day consent, the desire to live together, and the will to perpetuate the value of the heritage that one has received in an undivided form."[1] The case of a village, Slemence, in the former Subcarpatian area, and today divided between Slovakia and Ukraine, forces us to rethink the famous Renan questioning of the modern nation in a completely new way. The split occurred after Soviet troops entered Subcarpatian Ukraine in November 1944 and a Communist Party congress in Uzhhorod voted for it to become a part of the USSR. After the subsequent annexation of this territory by the Red Army on 29 June 1945, the closure of the border became permanent.[2]

Let us further delve into the European concept of nationhood; we find there is no Westoxification involved in the attempted narrative. Since the end of the Roman Empire or, better yet, since the breakup of Charlemagne's empire, western Europe has appeared to be divided into nations. These at certain moments, have sought to exercise hegemony over the others without ever having succeeded in a lasting fashion. What Charles V, Louis XIV, and Napoleon I were unable to do is likely that no one shall do in the future. The establishment of a new Roman or **Charlemagne** empire has become an impossibility.[3] The division of Europe has reached such a point that any attempt at universal domination quickly provokes a coalition that returns the ambitious nation to its natural frontiers. A sort of equilibrium has been long established. France, England, Germany, and Russia shall, for hundreds of years remain, and despite whatever they will have experienced in the meantime, historic individuals will remain like the essential pieces of a chequer board whose squares vary ceaselessly in importance and grandeur without ever fully being lost in one another. Understood in this way, nations are something rather new in history.[4] Antiquity did not know them: Egypt, China, and ancient Chaldea were in no sense nations. They were herds led by a child of the Sun or of the Sky. They were no Egyptian citizens, no more than there were Chinese ones. Classical antiquity had its republics and municipal kingdoms, its confederations of local republics, its empires. It hardly had a nation in the sense that we understand it. Athens, Sparta, Sidon, and Tyre were small centres of admirable patriotism but they were cities with relatively restrained territory.

Ernest Renan further contends that, "Prior to their absorption into the Roman Empire, Gaul, Spain, and Italy were assemblages of peoples, often comprising leagues between themselves but without central institutions or dynasties. The Assyrian, Persian, and Alexandrine empires also did not constitute fatherlands. There were never any Assyrian patriots; the Persian Empire was one great fief. Not a single nation finds its origins in Alexander's colossal adventure, otherwise so rich in consequences for the general history of civilization. The Roman Empire was much nearer to being a fatherland. In response to the cessation of wars, Roman domination, at first so hard, quickly came to be loved. It was a grand association synonymous with order, peace, and civilization. In the last days of the Empire, there was to be found among elevated souls, enlightened bishops and the presence of a genuine sentiment for the 'Roman peace' rather than one opposed to the menacing chaos of barbarous countries."[5]

The nationalist scholar further orated. "But, an empire twelve times the size of present-day France does not constitute a state in the modern sense of the word. The schism between the East and the West was inevitable. The attempts to found a Gallic empire in the third-century did not succeed. It was the Germanic invasions which introduced in the world the principle that, later on would come to serve as the basis for the existence of nationalities."[6]

Thus, as we can take cognizance from the acclaimed academic works of scholars working on the concept of nation-state and nationalism. The terminology of nationalism and the attendant perception of nationalism acts a substratum of the efficiency and effectiveness of a nation's foreign policy and its global outreach. The more the faith of the population in the ideals of nation state is, the more is the weight and impact of the nation's diplomacy and foreign policy in the global platforms. This is reflected in the regional organizations, too. International organizations of the order of BRICS, SCO, BIMSTEC and of course the entire paraphernaliac expanse of the United Nations are testimony to this fact. Thus, in the present Indian context of PM Narendra Modi's diplomacy, faith in the history, tradition, and cultural and classical verve of the Bharatiya civilization and not a mere nation, is the ideal which gets amply reflected in the narrative of Bharat's foreign policy since May 2014.

Thus, territoriality is an important cornerstone of the larger meaning of India's foreign policy. As an instance, during the Depsang and Galwan border row, the Indian Prime Minister crossed all diplomatic and foreign policy dogmas and launched forth the grand and muscular arm of Indian diplomacy. After the bloody border confrontation between Indian and Chinese forces, New Delhi declared its muscular overarch with the Prime Ministerial statement that India is prepared to tackle any misadventure by the Chinese and other vile antagonists. Thus, we can see that territorial allegiance, symbolism and their loss was once again interpolated as the sine quo non of India's foreign policy in the light of the confrontation with the hegemony by PRC.

A Brookings report can be factored into the contemporary context of the fundamental elements in the nation's foreign policy. Institutions such as Brookings completely wrote off the foreign policy segment and stand of Narendra Modi's electoral and domestic policy which was rather misplaced as all this circumspection was proven wrong by the manner in which the government handled the Galwan, Depsang and Balakot profligacy and malevolent interruptions. Brookings writes that "During the hustings last year, foreign policy was barely mentioned in Narendra Modi's campaign. However a year after his stunning victory, which gave India its first majority government in nearly 30 years, Prime Minister Modi has emerged as one of the most dynamic Indian and, indeed, international leader in the realm of foreign policy. The Indian Prime Minister has already notched an impressive list of foreign policy 'firsts': the first to invite leaders from the South Asian Association of Regional Cooperation (SAARC) countries to his swearing-in. New Delhi was the first to host an American president at the Republic Day celebrations and have two summits within six months; the first to call for 'peace, stability and order' in the oceans, outer space and cyber space. Bharat is the first to articulate the need for India to lead the fight against climate change and take responsibility to help counter new threats to global peace and security."[7]

The Brookings report further contends that, "In retrospect Mr. Modi's foreign policy activism is inevitable and is driven by the twin objectives of making India the world's third largest economy and, consequently, a key player in an emerging multipolar world. To achieve these objectives, two conditions are essential: first, ensuring a no-war scenario in the SAARC neighbourhood, which would make India an attractive destination for foreign investment and, second, developing the ability to shape the rules in global institutions, which will have a direct bearing on the country's economic well-being. These objectives are not new.

What has changed in Mr. Modi's stead has been the implementation and operationalization of some of the New Panchsheel in a more meaningful way to deepen and widen India's foreign policy engagement. The major thrust of Mr. Modi's foreign trips and bilateral engagements so far has been to attract investment and technology by reviving stalled ties with strategically important countries, such as the United States and France, and energizing decades-old neglected relationships with Japan, Australia, Germany and Canada."[8]

The report further elucidates that "This robust engagement led to Japan and France promising to invest 35 billion dollars and 2 billion Euros, respectively. The Chinese Premier Xi Jinping's September 2014 visit to India saw Beijing committing to invest 20 billion dollars in India over the next five years. Similarly, breakthroughs in agreements on civil nuclear cooperation with Canada and the USA further bolstered his foreign policy and economic agenda. Nonetheless, the sum of these investments is still only a fraction of the one trillion dollars that India estimates it needs for infrastructure alone."[9] This was the gloomy forecast of myriad Western observers and think tanks in such a manner which attempted to belittle the innovation and the new-found buoyancy of Indian foreign policy since May 2014. The trenchant strength and the well-meaning intent of New Delhi was initiated in 2014 which had gone flaccid since a long time in the New Delhi denomination. It is here that the elements of sovereignty, territoriality and sovereignty and public opinion once again re-entered and were ushered in by the New Delhi dispensation with a direct effloresce of the nation's foreign policy in the light of a world marred by the three-fold threats of the COVID epidemic, the Ukraine-Russia war and the au courant Israel-Hamas war and conflagration. Thus, the domestic roots of India's foreign policy assume a vital role in the deft and utilizable realization of an efficacious and meaningful role of India's foreign policy in the larger global firmament.

The Tenet of Non-Violence in Bharat's Foreign Policy

It can be succinctly argued that the non-violent tradition of India's freedom struggle can be understood as one of the fundamental determinants of the nation's foreign policy and diplomacy. Mahatma

Gandhi initiated the freedom struggle's non-violent phase against the might of the exploitative and suppressive British colonial rule. This was naturally embedded as the peacenik approach of a free and independent nation after 1947.

Emperor Ashoka abandoned war and conflict as an instrument of ancient India's foreign policy and this was aptly adhered to by the freedom fighters of the land. Though in the *Sanatana Dharma*, the exploits of power and conquest are extolled in the context of *raj dharma*. Preventive diplomacy has been the quintessential order of the order as far as the foreign policy and diplomacy of the nation is concerned. The hallowed governmental portal, Press Information Bureau, succinctly informs us that "The idea of neutrality or its use as a political precept is not unknown to India. The basic values that underlie the policy of neutrality are of peace, non-violence and peaceful resolution of disputes. This has remarkable similarities with the overall approach of the Non-Aligned Movement (NAM), the fundamental objective of the latter also being preservation of world peace and security, and of which Turkmenistan is now an active member. One of the cardinal principles of NAM was independence from great powers or bloc politics and rivalries. This did not imply a passive role for the movement in international politics but the formulation of positions in an independent manner so as to reflect the interests of its members."[10] Thus, it is not passivity or reactivity which is the tenet of India's external affairs policy but an idealistic espousal of peace, stability, sustainability and espousal of the lore of the peace tradition of *Sanatana Dharma*. This self-belief serves as one of the key bulwarks of the nation's foreign policy along with non-alignment and neutrality from the capitalist power bloc led by the United States of America and the socialistic bloc chaperoned by the erstwhile Soviet Union.

The PIB further informs us, "As one of the founding members of NAM, India has always taken a supportive position on Turkmenistan's neutrality. We have – both at bilaterally and international forums – conveyed our appreciation of the positive contribution made by this policy towards providing security, stability, sustainable development and humanitarian assistance in the region as well as the all-round progress of Turkmenistan."[11] It is naturally observed that weak nations have been known to proffer a policy paradigm of neutrality in the arena of world politics. They cannot apparently afford full-fledged warfare as it is beyond their delimited financial resources and commercial means.

Though such nations are known to carry out subterfuge and terror operations against their adversaries, the Islamic Republic of Pakistan does it clandestinely. Though India ought to be prepared for a two-and-a-half front war if the Chinese and the Pakistanis jointly militarily aggress against India and cause a half front of internal insurgencies to surmount India. Bharat has always opted for effective self-defence akin to its peace credentials. This is also the trail of thought and policy as often elucidated by India's External Affairs Minister, S. Jaishankar. Thus, non-violence serves as a standard requirement and a defining methodology of Bharat's foreign policy.

The Indian Foreign Minister recently declared in a jaunty declaration that much nearer home in the South-East Asian region, India vouches for peace, cooperation and mutual cooperation. Let us look into the contours of South-East Asia too. *The Economic Times* informs us that "The Mekong-Ganga Cooperation (MGC) is an initiative by six countries – India and five ASEAN countries, Cambodia, Lao PDR, Myanmar, Thailand, and Vietnam – for cooperation in tourism, culture, education, and transport and communications. Peace and prosperity in the region also play a pivotal role in realizing Prime Minister (Narendra) Modi's vision of security and growth for all in the region under India's Act East policy."[12] The national daily further informs that "Jaishankar said the meeting discussed prioritising the implementation of the India-Myanmar-Thailand Trilateral Highway and expediting the conclusion of the Motor Vehicles Agreement between the three countries.

Jaishankar further elaborated "that the establishment of a MGC Business Council to take forward economic cooperation and exploring new areas of development partnership, including through Quick Impact Projects, were also discussed. The meeting also discussed the expansion of "the ambit of exchanges in agriculture, science and technology and water resource management" and taking "forward culture and tourism, and deepening our museum-based cooperation." India and South-East Asian nations such as Cambodia, Indonesia and Malaysia share historically classical, civilizational and cultural roots with New Delhi. Still one can come across Hindu names like Ram Charan and Krishna Gopal in countries such as Indonesia. The fervent premise of this cultural togetherness happens to be enshrined in the peace tradition of PM Modi's foreign policy not only towards South-East Asia but through the ambit of the Act East Policy. The innovation lies in the fact that this peace approach to foreign policy and international cooperation is being extrapolated in the nation's transactions and image building in the larger part of the global system also.

It can be surmised that *Sanatana Dharma* forms the receptacle of world peace and sustainability as is observed by several IR scholars and followers of foreign policy. Chief Minister Yogi Adityanath has contended that only *Sanatana Dharma* guarantees peace and it is the reason why when there is a 'sankat' (trouble) in the world. Every country looks towards India and Prime Minister Narendra Modi. There is turmoil around the world, but the guarantee of world peace lies only in *Sanatana Dharma* and India. Whenever there is a 'sankat' or there is a global crisis, every country looks towards India and Prime Minister Narendra Modi with great hope. When 140 crore Indians come together behind this hope, it becomes a strength for the whole world.[13]

The Hindu University of America informs us that "This area enriches the discipline of conflict and peace studies by providing a Hindu perspective. By becoming more inclusive and pluralistic, conflicts at various levels can be approached more creatively. There are few contemporary studies on the Hindu perspective on conflict and peace. Most of these studies focus on the 20th century (particularly the latter half) Indian developments and juxtapose Indian thinking with dominant Western theories. The evolution of Hindu thought on these subjects, however, can be traced to the ancient period. One example would illustrate this point. India's national emblem is inscribed with the words '*Satyameva Jayate'* (Truth alone triumphs), which is from the ancient *Mundaka Upanichad*."[14]

The Hindu University of America's press release further informs us that "This area of studies, hence, while exploring the Hindu perspectives on violence, conflict, and wars, will examine their origins, and assess an innovative paradigm on peace-building. Notably, rigid compartmentalization of disciplines is foreign to traditional Hindu thinking, though most of the available studies in this area attempt to understand Indian scholarship through rigid disciplinary boundaries. Educational courses in this area of study can address this critical gap. They will examine various facets of conflict and peace, study existing scholarship and dominant theories in the discipline. They explore the ancient Hindu wisdom, empowering students to develop an integrated perspective on conflict resolution and peace-building and apply their understanding in creative ways to contemporary conflicts and challenges facing humanity."[15]

Thus, when we look askance towards the Western theme of peace studies and conflict resolution, we can feel a rarefied stream of proud and self-pontification that the idioms of *Sarva Dharma Sambhav* and *Vasudheva Kutumbakam*, stand for. It seems that the West and Occidental scholars and narratives might have taken leaves out of our peace studies and knowledge systems. Anyway, peace studies lies comfortably ensconced in our Bharatiya foreign policy thought as is evident in the large contingents of the Indian Army joining the United Nations Peace Keeping Forces the world over. At one point of time, India was proudly displaying its peace keepers, that is, the classical Blue Berets, as they are called, as a significant foreign policy achievement of Bharatvarsha in the immediate aftermath of India's political independence.

Thus, through adherence to the Indian scriptures, one can reach an educational and transformative element of the hallowed nation's foreign policy and diplomacy. Raj Kumar Dhungana of the Kathmandu University writes that "Hinduism is one of the most classical living religious/cultural groups of the world with a following of nearly 900 million people. Modern education has left the classical knowledge behind and looking for new avenues for a better future. Vedic Hindu ideology depicted in the Vedas, Upanishads, the *Ramayana*, and the *Mahabharata* are rich in the emancipatory knowledge that the 'whole world is one family' and advancing people to be cosmic citizens by widening their narrow self."[16] Thus, the peaceable nature and the singularly and overtly vegetative approach of India's foreign policy bring us back to the fundamental peaceful premise of the nation's external relations. Our scriptures form an essential base and foundation of how non-violence still remains the driving force behind how India tackles its arch adversaries and allies and partners alike. It is here that lies the true-blue value of Bharatvarsha's approach to world turmoil and turbulence in the larger global context.

Geography as a Key Factor

C. Rajamohan writes in *Crossing the Rubicon* that, "India lies at an interesting and critical geo strategic cusp in the world system. The South Asian nation serves as a connecting element between the Central Asian region and the Asia–Pacific."[17] India is the pivot regionally and globally too. Ambassador Rajiv Sikri writes that "Indians developed a defensive mindset. They did not craft a strategy to tackle foreign threats. The limited problems of diplomacy and statecraft involved ambitious feuding rulers within the Indian subcontinent. India did not have clearly defined borders. Rather, it had frontier zones – in the northwest, the Himalayas and in the northeast. These were left alone, as long as they did not threaten the security of the heartland. Invariably, these zones had as extensive contacts with India as with areas on the other side, namely, Afghanistan, Tibet and Burma."[18] India, boasted of the natural motifs of the order of the Young Himalayas, the Indian Ocean's maritime comfort. The presence of weaker nations such as Myanmar, Afghanistan and Tibet in the near neighbourhood, could breathe easy in the recent and the medieval historical past.

The MEA release further informs us that "In today's world, India's geography poses three principal foreign policy challenges. One, whereas the modern Indian state requires fixed, determinable borders, the inhabitants of these amorphous frontier zones have traditionally had, and do indeed need, flexible borders. Trying to demarcate a historically non-existent border gives rise to border disputes as, for example, with

China. Two, today's political borders of South Asia are artificial. India has been divided in the past, but never so irrationally as it has been since 1947. India's neighbours want to keep their distance from India in order to assert and preserve their sovereignty. Thus they deliberately downplay their interdependence, complementarities and commonalities with India. At the same time, they can ignore neither the tugs of a shared history and culture, nor the compulsions of intertwined economic and social ties."[19] One can definitely talk in terms of nebulous and ambiguous frontiers akin to the American Wild West where the international boundaries are not demarcated and delineated leading to border war. the Chinese LOAC and the LOC with Pakistan being pertinent examples which serve as posers to the nation's foreign policy.

The MEA release carries on in the same informative vein that "Three, India is boxed in by Pakistan on the west and Bangladesh on the east. Without their cooperation, India cannot meaningfully extend its overland reach and influence. At the same time, India is very strategically located in the heart of Asia and dominates the Indian Ocean, which is named after India. It was from India (which the British regarded as 'the jewel in the crown') that the mighty British Empire controlled the whole of Asia. East Africa, the Arab world, Central Asia and Southeast Asia are all within easy reach of India. The main sea lines of communication in the Indian Ocean pass very close to India. The Persian Gulf, which is the principal source of exportable global oil and gas, is India's neighbour. Unfortunately, terrorism, fundamentalism, piracy and narcotics production are rampant in areas that surround India."[20] Thus, in more than one manner, the geography of the Indian nation serves as a paramount determinant of the nation's foreign policy in all its probable permutations and combinations. This safe encasement led Bharat to reside in an ivory tower which was furthered by the protection of the might and pelf of the British Empire. The technological advancements and the fall from grace and power of the British Empire became the hard realities of the day in the aftermath of World War II. Then as a related development, the nation had to confront warplanes, intercontinental ballistic missiles, and radar and war aviation; now drone swarms which have compromised the protection offered to the Indian nation.

The Concerns of Sovereignty

When a nation assumes statehood, it becomes pertinent that the government of the land becomes the sole interpreter and the only executing and implementing agency. According to the works of the Social Contract theorists, when they talk about Thomas Hobbes, then at that piquant point of time, the citizens of the nation surrender all their rights to the sovereign ruler, the Leviathan.[21] Only the right to self-defence and survival rests with the denizens of the nation. Once this glorious sacrifice has been made, then at that point of time, the sovereign rules the roost. In the work of John Locke's *The Second Treatise on Government*, the government takes away all rights from the denizens of the nation and only the right to liberty, happiness, contentment and survival are wished away by the government of the day.[22]

Still, in a strictly stereotypical tradition of democracy and governance, the argument can be advanced that it is the people and their opinion which form the body politique of the sovereign ruler. The lives and rights of the subjects might be compromised for the sovereign rule book or the Constitution, the commonality and the conjoined nature of the subjects. Thus, the ruler or the sovereign cannot be ruled out or pushed under the carpet in the larger narrative on nationalism and nationhood. The same all-pervasive power of the ruler or the sovereign ought to be the order of the day. All in all, it can be argued that the king ought to be the final and ultimate authority in a nation-state with command of the external affairs department with the all-pervasive and non-subservient right to declare war.

Thus, the commandeering authority of the land can make or mar the lives of the antagonist states. Still, the legitimacy of the sovereign or the form of government in the nation, ought never be questioned, either domestically or internationally. There should be unanimity in the global comity of states that the actual centre of legitimacy and authority lie in the nation-state. In the context of Pakistan, an overture by New Delhi has to be met by the capacity of tackle the Deep State of the Islamic Republic of Pakistan.

Let us delve into the factoid that the Inter-Services Intelligence of Pakistan, the Rawalpindi headquarters of the Pakistan army, along with the fundamentalist coterie of terror-mongering Islamists claim recourse to real and actual authority in the pecking order of power in Pakistan. A nation like India needs to be crystal clear as to who is New Delhi altercating and playing diplomacy with. Thus arises the reflected significance of the sovereign of the land. Also, as an attendant fact, non-state actors such as the Taliban have transformed themselves into rulers of the Afghani badlands. Now, how does a beleaguered External Affairs Minister of India, Jaswant Singh, confabulate with the Foreign Minister of Kabul, who travels in a Toyota SUV and carries a missile launcher in his car? Can the twilight zone nature of non-state actors be equated with their being branded as insurgents and separatists in order to keep the tenet of the nation-state alive and kicking.

Jonathan Ian White writes that "The intellectual history of sovereignty has created and maintained a hierarchy in international relations, to the extent that the theory and practice of statehood is 'colonized' through latent ethnocentric and a priori assumptions. The ontological foundations of sovereign statehood as existing in the thought of Hobbes, creates, inherently, a normative hierarchy in which those that exist outside the zone of European enlightenment are 'othered'. In practice, this hierarchy is visible in contemporary and historical intervention in the Global South. Historically, formal colonialism was justified on the grounds that those in the Orient were in need of the properties of European civilization. This rested on the ontological assumption that outside the Western state system, exists an anarchical 'zone of otherness' as articulated in the thought of Hobbes. It is worth noting that there has been an essential continuity in the construction of the relations between the Orient and the Occident. With respect to this, interventionism today is justified under the assumption that the West is the sole protector of human rights in international relations."[23]

A prevailing fallacy in the literature is to place the Peace of

Westphalia at the centre of the emergence of the international sovereign state system. For example, Morgenthau states that "the rules of international law were securely established in 1648". Similarly, Boucher supposes that Westphalia "provided the foundation for, and gave formal recognition to, the modern states system." This narrative is so ubiquitous that quotes such as these can be "multiplied at will".[24] However, it is factually problematic. On one level, as Osiander points out, there is nothing explicit in the treaties of Munster and Osnabruck which codify the principles that we know as Westphalian Sovereignty. It is certain that the participants of the negotiations "did not see themselves establishing a new political entity called 'the state'."[25] Similarly, the narrative that the post-Westphalian world was one defined by a reification of the principle of non-intervention (that is, that the treaties were a 'watershed' moment in the history of international relations) is pure fallacy. As Finnemore contends, "There was plenty of military activity across the borders to change rulers in this period, but people called it war".[26] Considering the inconsistencies in the 'Westphalian narrative' the f is that it's somewhat intellectually dubious to attribute such a wide-reaching principle to a singular set of treaties. It is more credible to conceptualise the emergence of the sovereign state order as an ideological struggle rather than as a discrete phenomenon of the Peace of Westphalia. With respect to that, the prevailing ideological underpinnings of sovereign principles can be traced to the fifteenth and sixteenth century European political thought.[27]

Today, New Delhi's contemporary diplomatic establishment too does not relate much and adhere to the notion of nation-states as elucidated and brought into currency through the tenets of the Treaty of Westphalia. India too had its sub nations which were regularized by provincial nations of the order of Licchavi, which were cobbled together by great emperors of the order of Ashoka, Pushyamitra Shunga, Harshvardhan and Pulkeshin. Thus, when one delves into the tenets of sovereignty and international relations, one might not completely be overawed by the initial construct as propounded by a Eurocentric Treaty of Westphalia. India too, had its own idea of nationhood which was traversed and practiced adroitly by the Mauryan, Gupta and Shunga dynasties in the ancient age of the Indic nation-state.

Sovereignty is a type of authority relationship. Despite the volumes written about it, authority is one of those terms like power that political scientists, and especially those in international relations, define only with difficulty. Definition, authority is a social relationship in which 'A (a person or occupant of an office) wills B to follow A and B voluntarily complies'. In other words, authority is characterized by commands issued by an actor that are expected to be obeyed by a second party.[28] In a manner, one may argue in an outlandish manner that power, including the ides of a well orchestrated game of IR and IO, can define sovereignty in the context of the larger Asiatic space and the larger context of South Asia.

One might conveniently observe that India's foreign policy under Prime Minister Narendra Modi is akin to the power approach of public diplomacy. The Indian Prime Minister adheres to a muscular, aggressive and proactive paradigm in external relations, wherein, the region and the concept of a larger Bharatvarsha holding sway over the entire Indian subcontinent can be creatively alluded to. Thus, the tit for tat IR game is being assiduously followed by the Indian Prime Minister wherein the idiom of being forceful and organic in one's approach driven entirely by our national interests has become the Indian credo in both Modi 1.0 and 2.0.

According to Neorealist scholar Krachowick, "Structural questions are questions about the arrangement of the parts of a system. The parts of domestic political systems stand in relations of super- and sub-ordination. Domestic systems are centralized and hierarchic. The parts of international political-systems stand in relations of coordination. Formally, each is the equal of all the others. International systems are decentralized and anarchic."[29] Thus, in the Indian context, the New Delhi dispensation has gone ahead and contemplated that as anarchy, disarray and heady and potent pandemonium rules the roost in the Indian neighbourhood India has taken up the mantle of the regional leader perched with the IMEC (India Middle East Corridor) countering the Belt and Road Initiative of the Chinese strategy. Thus, New Delhi has assumed the mantle of regional and South-Asian leadership making it confront the Chinese façade of peaceful rise in more ways than one.

Idea of Sovereignty and the Indian Perspective: The *Mandala*, *Shukraniti* Narrative

Not many concepts and idioms are a maze akin to the concept of sovereignty, wherein the entity of reason leads us to the genuine philosophical meaning of the concept. It not been, from the very start, sufficiently examined and seriously tested by them. The question was asked whether the international community as a whole is not the true holder of sovereignty, rather than the individual states. Besides, in some quarters, the very notion of sovereignty was challenged.[30]

Jean Bodin contended that the emperor did not have super powers to decide unilaterally about sovereignty, a sovereignty that has absolutely nothing above itself; God was above the king, and the supreme power of the king over his subjects was itself subservient to 'the law of God and nature.' Thus, Bodin's position is perfectly clear. When Jean Bodin says that the sovereign prince is the image of God, this phrase must be understood in its full force, and means that the sovereign submitted to God, but was accountable only to Him, transcends the political whole just as God transcends the cosmos.[31]

The Legislator, that superman described in the *Contract Social*, written by Rousseau offers us a preview of our modern totalitarian dictators, whose "great soul is the true miracle which should prove" their 'mission,' and who have to "alter man's constitution in order to strengthen it."[32] Rousseau's State was but the Hobbesian Leviathan, crowned with the General Will.[33] It ought to be ascertained and aptly released that rulers who rule with amalgamated governance policy of stick-and-rod need to be reprimanded. Also, as an attendant fact, in the Bharatiya context, PM Modi's manner of functioning has been derided by the political opposition as a kind of autocratic and totalitarian way of execution and functioning. Some stray voices in PM Modi's ruling clique too made such noises during the initial segment of Modi 1.0.

Coming back to the notion of Indic IR, the Hindu theory of sovereignty did not stop, however, at the doctrine of a universal *Matsya-Nyaya*, that is, of a world in which each state is at war with all. It generated also the concept of universal peace through the establishment of a Weltherrschaft as in Dante's *De Monarchia*. The doctrine of *mandala* as a centrifugal force was counteracted by the centripetal tendencies of the doctrine of *sarva-bhauma* (the ruler over the whole Earth). To this theory of the world state, we shall now address ourselves. In Europe, the idea or ideal of a universal empire took most definite shape towards the beginning of the fourteenth century. This crisis and this transition in Western political thought are best represented by Bartolus (1314-1357), the 'prince of jurists,' for he began by seeing a single universal empire, but, he ended by recognizing a miniature empire in every de facto independent power. The same conception of a world sovereignty or a federation de l'empire is however as old in India as the political philosophers of the earliest Vedic period.

The doctrine of *Sarva-Bhauma* expressed the more popular and conventional conception of *Samrat* or the grandiloquent *Vijigisu*. The *Mahabharata*, for instance, uses this category in order to convey the idea of a world dominion. "There are rajas (kings) in every home (state) doing what they like," we read in the *Book on Sabha*, "but they have not attained to the rank of *samrat*; for that title is hard to win." This rank is at last won by Yudhisthira in the epic. Yudhisthira would thus be the Veltro of the *Divine Comedy*. Another category in which the doctrine of *sarva-bhauma* is manifest is that of *chatooranta*, of which Kautilya availed himself in order to establish his ideal of imperial nationalism. The *chatooranta* state is that whose authority extends up to the remotest *antas* (limits) of the *chatoor* (four) quarters. The ruler of such a state *ananyamprithiveembhoomkte*, that is, enjoys the whole Earth with none to challenge his might. In the *Artha-shastra*, he is known also as *chakravarti*, for the territory of such a *chatooranta* is called *chakravartiksetra* (dominion of a *chakravarti*).

Idea of Just War in Indic IR

While the nature of war and warfare has changed enormously over time, debates about whether, and in what circumstances, war can be justified have a much more enduring character. This dates back to ancient Rome and including medieval European philosophers such as Augustine of Hippo (354–430) and Thomas Aquinas.[34] The defining feature of political realism, sometimes referred to as realpolitik, is that matters of war and peace are beyond morality in that they are – and should be – determined by the pursuit of national self-interest.

The Just War theory addresses two separate but related issues. The first of these deals with the right to go to war in the first place, or what in Latin is called *jus ad bellum.*[35] The second deals with the right conduct of warfare, or what in Latin is called *jus in bello*.[36] Although these branches of Just War thinking complement one another and they may have quite different implications. For example, a state fighting for a just cause may use unjust methods. Nevertheless, it is unclear whether for a war to be just, it must fulfil all the conditions of *jus ad bellum* and *jus in bello*.

Ritualizing violence in literature along these lines might be analysed as one way of solving moral problems connected with the ethics of war. In a recent essay on the ethics of war in Hinduism, Francis X. Clooney points out that sacrificial violence is generally justified because it is required by the Vedas, whereas killing for mundane goals is always forbidden.[37] According to the dominant ethical traditions of Hinduism. George von Simson has argued that the *Mahabharata* reveals a certain ambiguity when it deals with points of fighting and killing that violate basic Hindu ideas of *jus in bello*, proper conduct in battle.

It seems that the Brahmins who have told and retold the story through the ages have sought ways to overcome the moral inconsistencies in the text. The contextualization of the war as a sacrifice solves this ethical problem by saying that all the belligerents of the epic in a sense agree on the choreography of this violent ritual. Furthermore, we might add that by conflating ideas of sacrifice and war, the Hindu world developed its very own version of the holy war. In particular, the idea of holy war is apparent when the central characters of the epic talk about the role of Krishna in the fighting. To Krishna, war is a game. As the high god, he is beyond moral considerations. At the same time, the active participation of Krishna in the battle guarantees the righteousness of Arjuna's cause.

PM Modi in the contemporary context does not refer to any holy war but a kind of idealistic notion of Just War. After innumerable negotiations and confabulations with antagonistic states, if peace does not prevail then a muscular foreign policy approach might be what the doctor ordered. PM Modi does not adhere to the American notion of the USA being the citadel on Mount Sinai but vouches for a higher perch of morality and ethics which is very much a much deliberated segment of India's foreign policy. Still, as has been observed, India talks about the concept of Vishwaguru and thus usurps and allocates for itself the higher and superior mantle of Bhạratiya sovereignty. In a manner, the higher ethical ground in the context of the interventionist zeal of the United States of America has been decried in international law and the larger comity of states. Still, Bharat with its pacific and peace approach has extolled a balancing act along with a non-hostile foreign policy approach which seeks global camaraderie and peaceful global intent as part of the constituents of the Bharatiya idiom of superior sovereignty. This peacenik approach is much different from the American hegemonising and expansive strategies.

Once the canard of the Chinese hegemony and expansiveness has been revealed, no longer does the international system believe in the Chinese rationale of its 'Peaceful Rise' which has always been guided by Xi Jinping's declared policy of, 'Hide your powers, bide your time, until you are powerful and stealthy enough'. After all, diplomacy is all about intelligence, tact, subterfuge and propaganda which are the unofficial and the under-the-table modus operandi of Bharat's or any other nation's foreign policy that supreme sovereignty has become in the 21st century. And, amplification it in a positive manner.

Further on: It's Geography

Jawaharlal Nehru has said, "India is located at a curious cusp wherein India in South Asia acts as a connective corridor with Central Asia in the north to South Asia. And, the larger Orient in the east. India has historically served as a bridge between two continents." Thus, India is straddled by the young Himalayas in the northern periphery and the oceanic moat of the Bay of Bengal and the Indian Ocean along with the Middle Eastern sway of the Arabian Sea. The Shakas and Hunas along with others like Alexander, Nadir Shah and Ghazni found it difficult to pierce through the northern geospatial protection ring of the nation which survived before leading on to get rid of the British colonial rule in the 20th century.

The border between India and China is chequered and it becomes the order of the day to delve into the relief features on the LOAC. Whether it's the northern section of the India-China border in and around Ladakh or NEFA (North Eastern Frontier Agency), the geographical features determine manifold border encampments and transgressions of the PLA. India and China share the longest disputed border in the world but no bullet was fired in nearly 50 years until the 15 June Galwan valley incident.

Geographically both the nations are contiguous to each other wherein China has been historically known to go ahead with a mapped or cartographic invasion of India apart from the border war of 1962. *Al Jazeera* reports, "Both countries claim vast swathes of each other's territory along the Himalayan frontier, with the border problems rooted in the demarcation of boundaries by British colonial rulers. The border can be grouped into three different sectors: Eastern, Central and Western. Beijing has never recognised the 1914 border drawn by British officer Henry McMahon. China currently claims 90,000 square kilometres (34,750 square miles) of territory – nearly all of which constitutes India's Arunachal Pradesh State. Beijing shows it as southern Tibet in its maps. On the other hand, India claims 38,000 sq km (15,000 sq miles) of land currently under Chinese control, which includes the Aksai Chin plateau near the Ladakh region."[38]

Geography and cartographic incursions by the Han have always had a kind of perpetually bedevilled relationship between both the nations, highlighting the geography as a prominent and determining factor. This tenet tends to destabilize the bilateral interactions between New Delhi and Beijing. Observer Research Foundation reports, "The five incidents reported in the Western sector of the border in 2013 had a geographical spread across the entire Ladakh-Tibet Autonomous region boundary. Incidents covered the span ranging from the northernmost end of the Indian border in Ladakh at Daulat Beg Oldi to its southernmost end at

Chumar; the maximum number of incidents reported in the middle sector in a single year was three in 2012. These three were the only ones during the entire period of 2003 to 2014 in this sector (Table 1). All were aerial incidents that occurred over the state of Himachal Pradesh. A report in the *Indian Express* said that the then Chief Minister of the state, Prem Kumar Dhumal, informed the Centre about the violations by Chinese helicopters entering Indian airspace along the international border on 16 March.

The ORF reports further pithily informs us, "Both the Indian Express and the Times of India quoted former Uttarakhand Chief Minister Vijay Bahuguna claiming that between 2006 and 2011, at least 37 incursions by Chinese forces occurred along the 350-km border that Uttarakhand shares with China. According to Bahuguna, there were six incursions in 2006, two in 2007, 10 in 2008, 11 in 2009, five in2010 and three in 2011. In contrast, for the corresponding period (2006-2011) there were no incidents reported in the newspapers in the middle sector."[39]

Table 1: Number of Incidents Reported and the Unique Incidents by Year According to Newspapers

Year	*Number of Incident Reports*			*Number of Unique Incidents*
	The Times of India	*Indian Express*	*The Hindu*	
2003-2005	2	0	0	2
2006-2008	3	2	2	4
2009-2011	8	5	4	8
2012-2014	14	15	13	16
Total	27	22	19	30

Thus, the menace of incursions remains a perennial bugbear for India wherever it shares its borders with the People's Republic of China. The debate in India is that despite India being a democracy the actual number, and nature and extent of the Chinese border and geographical incursions remains a perpetual incertitude. As far as geography as a determinant of the India-China fracas is concerned, the dark curtain remains unchallenged and unquestioned under the garb of ISR (Intelligence, Surveillance and Reconnaissance).

Alfred Thayer Mahan believed that the policy of a state lies in its geography. He stated, "But what is geography, after all? Whatever the answer, it is important first to make clear that Napoleon's expedient and sibylline formula is as unacceptable now as his foreign policy was then. This is true even if we conceive of geography as something more than topographical configurations or contrasts of climate. Napoleon himself, unlike the majority of authors who deal with international relations, had enough strategic experience and political realism to conceive of geography in less restricted and elementary terms. More than anyone, however, he had to realize that a state's foreign policy also derives from the ideas, the aspirations, and even the fantasies, of those who lead it, and particularly the one who leads. It is true that these ideas, these geopolitical projects, draw on geographic images that are to a greater or lesser degree subjective and deformed by ambition."[40]

The author further asserts that nevertheless, it is safe to assume that Yves Lacoste was the director of the Institute of Geography at the University of Paris VIII and editor of the review *Hérodote, ajournai* of geography and geopolitics. When Emperor Napoleon, master of most of Europe, plainly and with deliberate simplicity proclaimed his geographic formula (emphasizing both the topographical relief and the boundaries of the territories in his path); his purpose was to impose his geopolitical plan and present it as if it corresponded to the 'nature of things. Today still, recourse to geographic 'evidence' and 'imperatives' to justify the foreign policy of a state, is, a means of deflecting more complicated and less favourable analyses of that state's interests and ambitions. Another, more recent, example of the sort of political argument that appears to be based on geographic 'evidence' dates from the turn of the century. This was the time when Adm. Alfred Thayer Mahan and the geographer Halford Mackinder developed the famous theses of the fundamental antagonism between sea power and continental power, an opposition of land and sea that was alleged to date from antiquity.

Mackinder and Mahan spared nothing in their long descriptions of England's struggle with Napoleon. At the time they were developed, these theses corresponded to definite strategies. In the aftermath of World War II, they have had a considerable following because of the rivalry of the two superpowers, of which the Soviet Union is supposed to be the 'continental power' par excellence. Now that the number and tonnage of the Soviet submarine force is greater than the US Navy's and can easily pass under the ice barrier that surrounds Russia's major sea front, this appraisal will have to be revised."[41]

The author further asserts that "The theses of Mahan and Mackinder, to which today's geopoliticians attach too much importance, rest more on historical evocations than on rigorous strategic thinking. They are actually based on the grandiose geographic metaphors of the land and the sea. Although the theses lack scientific value, their lyrical function is unquestionable."[42] Thus, historically speaking, political geography has already taken its toll on the idiom of foreign relations and diplomacy in the old, classical and contemporary context too. One can safely argue that the land power idiom along with air power and sea expanse tenets have all got to do with the understanding and comprehension of the geography as a factor in forging new bonds or manoeuvring against potential and future antagonists.

The *American Political Science Review* informs us that "La politique de toutes les puissances est dans leur géographie," conceded the man whose famous retort, "Circonstances? Moi, je fais les circonstances," indicates his contempt for any agency but the human will as the arbiter of human destiny. But since the Red Sea parted for Moses and the sun obligingly paused for Joshua, the human will has been unable to recapture the control over topography and climate exhibited by those forceful gentlemen. It is probably safe to say that it was by Russian geography rather than by men that the diminutive Corsican was finally defeated. If he is still living, there is at Waterloo even today a loyal guide who asserts with unshakable conviction that neither genius nor skill but a swampy ditch gave that victory to Wellington."[43]

The thought further enlightens us that "Unfortunately for the political scientist with a fondness for simplification, but fortunately for the statesman striving to overcome the geographic handicaps of his country, neither does the entire foreign policy of a country lie in geography, nor does any part of that policy lie entirely in geography. The factors that condition the policy of states are many; they are permanent and temporary, obvious and hidden. They include, apart from the geographic factor, population density, the economic structure of the country, the ethnic composition of the people, the form of government, and the complexes and pet prejudices of foreign ministers. It is their simultaneous action and interaction that create the complex phenomenon known as "foreign policy'."[44] Though, we have been talking and researching and narrating with great aplomb about the geographic factors, still one need not overemphasize the clout of geography as an overriding factor in the diplomatic thought of the nations. It has been rightly and cogently pointed out that in the age of digitisation, digitalization and modernisation, the 20th century sways along with industrialization and the all-pervasive significance of air power. Drone swarms form the pertinent poser for the geography as a factor in a nation's foreign policy.

NOTES

1. Jana Dudkova. 'The Slovak Film: The Border and the Problem of the Creation of the Collective Identities,' URL https://src-h.slav.hokudai.ac.jp/pdf_seminar/ 20100927_ Dudkova2.pdf (Online: Web), accessed on 10 October 2023.
2. Ernest Renan. 'What is a Nation?' (1882), available at URL http://www.cooper.edu/ humanities/core/hss3/e_renan.html. (Online: Web), accessed on 10 October 102023.
3. Ernest Renan. 'What is a Nation?' Text of a lecture delivered at the Sorbonne on 1 March 1882, in Ernest Renan, 'Qu'est-ce qu'une nation?' Paris, Presses-Pocket, 1992. (translated by Ethan Rundell).
4. Ibid.
5. Ibid. Fn. 1.
6. Ibid., Fn. 2.
7. W.P.S. Sandhu & Vikram Singh Mehta, 'Modi's Foreign Policy at the rate of 365: Course Correction,' Brookings Report, May, 2016.
8. Ibid.
9. Ibid. 1, Fn. 1.
10. Press Information Bureau. Vice President's Address, (Online: Web), URL, https://pib. gov.in/newsite/PrintRelease.aspx?relid=133127#:~:text=Friends%2C-,The% 20idea% 20of%20neutrality%20or%20its%20use%20as%20a%20political,and%20 peaceful % 20resolution%20of%20disputes, (Online: Web), accessed on 10 November 2023.
11. Ibid.
12. Press Trust of India. 'Peace and Tranquility in the Mekong Region', *The Economic Times*, 16 July 2003.

13. Express News Service. 'Sanatan Dharma Guarantees World Peace,' *Indian Express*, 13 October 2023.
14. 'Hindu University of America,' URL https://www.hua.edu/academics/areas-of-study/conflict-and-peace-studies/ (Online: Web), accessed on 10 October 2023.
15. Ibid.
16. Raj Kumar Dhungana. *Peace Education: A Hindu Perspective*, Palgrave, New Delhi, 2013.
17. C. Rajamohan. *India's Foreign Policy: Crossing the Rubicon*, Penguin, India, 2008.
18. Ambassador Rajiv Sikri. 'India's Foreign Policy: Determinants, Issues and Challenges,' Ministry of External Affairs, Govt. of India, 13 February 2017.
19. Ibid.
20. Ibid., Fn. 1.
21. Thomas Hobbes. *The Leviathan*, Penguin Classics, London, 1971.
22. John Locke. *The Second Treatise on Government*, Penguin Classics, London, 1978.
23. Jonathan Ian White. 'A Critical Reflection on Sovereignty in International Relations Today,' URL https://www.e-ir.info/2019/02/09/a-critical-reflection-on-sovereignty-in-international-relations-today/ (Online: Web), accessed on 11 September 2023.
24. Osiander, A. (2001). 'Sovereignty, International Relations, and the Westphalian Myth.' *International Organization*, [online] 55(2), pp. 251-287. Available at: https://www.cambridge.org/core/journals/international-organization/article/sovereignty-international-relations-and-the-westphalian-myth/33B6B7773432BE494F31518952ABE881, accessed on 10 November 2018.
25. Havercroft, J. (2012). 'Was Westphalia 'all that'? Hobbes, Bellarmine, and the norm of non-intervention' *Global Constitutionalism*, [online] 1(01), pp. 120-140, available at: https://www.cambridge.org/core/journals/global-constitutionalism/article/was-westphalia-all-that-hobbes-bellarmine-and-the-norm-of-nonintervention/0B95A1A6DCB6ED6C8CD1FA022C532B3B
26. Finnemore, M. (2003). *The Purpose of Intervention*, New York, Cornell University Press, p. 10.
27. Ibid.
30. David A. Lake, 'The New Sovereignty in International Relations,' *International Studies Review,* 2003, pp. 302 323.
28. Ibid.
29. Kratochwil, Friedrich. (1989) *Rules, Norms, and Decisions: On the Conditions of Practical and Legal Reasoning in International Relations and Domestic Affairs*, New York, Cambridge University Press.
30. Ibid.
31. A. Dunning. 'Jean Bodin on Sovereignty,' P*olitical Science Quarterly*, vol. 11, no. 1 (March 1896), pp. 82-104.
32. Dr. Arvind Adityaraj. 'Why Rosseau Developed the Theory of Sovereignty,' B A Part One study material, Patna University, India.
33. Jean Jacques Rousseau. *Confessions The Social Contract Discourse on Inequality Discourse on Political Economy & Discourse on the Effect of the Arts and Sciences on Morality*, Benediction Classics, 2019.
34. George Holland Sabine. *A History of Political Theory*, Benediction Classics, 1970.
35. Andrew Heywood. *Politics*, New York, Palgrave Macmillan, 2014.

36. Ibid.
37. Francis X. Clooney. *Reading the Hindu and Christian Classics: Why and How It Matters,* University of Virginia Press, 2019.
38. 'World's Longest Disputed Border,' URL https://interactive.aljazeera.com/aje/2020/mapping-india-and-china-disputed-borders/index.html (Online Web), accessed in December 2022.
39. Ibid.
40. Yves Lacoste. 'Geography and Foreign Policy,' *SAIS Review*, John Hopkins University Press, vol.4, no. 2, Fall, 1984.
41. Ibid.
42. Ibid. Fn. 1.
43. Nicholas J. Spykman. 'Geography and Foreign Policy', *American Political Science Review*, February 1938.
44. Ibid.

Chapter Three

India-Pak Relations as Shooting Wars

Salman Rushdie described India-Pakistan relations and the culture of Kashmir as a 'palimpsest' wherein the denizens sustained as a kind of commonly shared society and comity of hoi polloi. The beauty of Kashmir was flowered and initialised by Hindu rulers wherein the population and the canvas of culture came to fruition through the conjoined Wazwan culture and the amalgamated credo. Pakistan was born as a progeny of the transfer of power and the Partition which bloodied and tarred the scheme of affairs in the beautiful valley of the Gods. The idiom of the two-nation theory subsisted as the nom de plume of the fundamentals of the twin neighbours. Both the neighbours have fought four wars with each other since the attainment of independence from the British colonial rule.

India has followed a consistent and principled policy towards Pakistan, that is, in keeping with its 'Neighbourhood First Policy'. India seeks normal neighbourly relations with Pakistan in an environment free from terror, hostility and violence. India is committed to address issues, if any, bilaterally and peacefully in keeping with the Simla Agreement and the Lahore Declaration. India will not compromise on issues related to its national security and take firm and decisive measures to deal with all attempts to undermine India's security and territorial integrity.

Striving for Engagement

The Indian High Commission in Pakistan informs us that "India has made a number of attempts to build normal neighbourly relations with Pakistan. Since 2014, this has manifested in the invitation to the then Prime Minister Nawaz Sharif for the swearing-in ceremony in May 2014; the meeting between prime ministers in Ufa in July 2015; and the External Affairs Minister's (EAM) visit to Islamabad in December 2015. The EAM also took the initiative to propose a comprehensive bilateral dialogue in December 2015. These initiatives have been responded with acts of cross-border terrorism and violence against India including the cross-border terror attack on the Pathankot airbase on 2 January 2016; attack on an army camp in Uri in August 2016."[1]

The report further narrates that "Prime Minister spoke to Mr. Imran Khan on 30 July 2018 and congratulated him for his party emerging as the largest political party in the National Assembly. The PM also sent a congratulatory letter to PM Imran Khan on 18 August 2018 desiring meaningful and constructive engagement for the benefit of the people of the entire region. The EAM congratulated the new Foreign Minister on 22 August 2018. In response to the PM's congratulatory letter, Pakistan wrote back on 14 September 2018 and suggested a meeting between foreign ministers in UNGA in New York. The new foreign minister of Pakistan also wrote to the EAM on 17 September 2018 with a similar proposal. These letters mentioned bringing a positive change and mutual desire for peace, and also Pakistan's readiness to discuss terrorism."[2]

The report further posits that "In response to the intentions expressed in these letters, Pakistan's proposal for a meeting was accepted by India on 20 September 2018. However, within hours of India's acceptance, Pakistan-based terrorist entities brutally killed three police personnel in the state of Jammu and Kashmir. Earlier, that same week, an Indian BSF soldier was brutally killed at the border on 18 July 2018. All these incidents happened after Pakistan's PM and FM wrote letters to India's leadership expressing their desire for change and for peace."[3] Moreover, India's strong protests with Pakistan and call for remedial action were met with outright denial. Under such circumstances, it was assessed that any conversation with Pakistan would be meaningless. India was left with no choice but to call off the meeting between the foreign ministers of India and Pakistan in New York.

PM Modi received a telephone call from the Pakistan PM on 26 May 2019 congratulating him on his election victory. PM Modi thanked him and recalled his earlier suggestion to the Pakistan PM to fight poverty jointly. PM Modi also stressed that creating trust and an environment free of violence and terrorism were essential for fostering cooperation for peace, progress and prosperity in the region.[4] Pakistan is yet to respond like a normal neighbour. It has continued to restrict even normal trade and connectivity with India. On 7 August 2019, Pakistan regrettably took unilateral action to downgrade diplomatic relations with India in an attempt to present an alarming picture of bilateral ties to the world. India has urged Pakistan to review its unilateral actions in respect of relations with India so that normal channels of diplomatic communications, are, preserved.

Cross-border Terrorism

Terrorism emanating from territories under Pakistan's control remains a core concern in bilateral relations. India has consistently stressed the need for Pakistan to take credible, irreversible and verifiable action to end cross-border terrorism against India and fulfil its assurances, given to India at the highest level in January 2004 and reiterated several times. It has been reiterated that territory under its control would not be allowed to be used for terrorism against India in any manner.

India has repeatedly called upon Pakistan to bring the perpetrators of the Mumbai terror attacks to justice expeditiously. However, there has been no progress in the ongoing trial of the Mumbai terror attacks case in Pakistan even after all the evidence has been shared with Pakistan. It has also been emphasised that India will continue to take firm and decisive steps to protect its national security. Following the cross-border terrorist attack on an army camp in Uri in Jammu and Kashmir on 18 September 2016, the Indian Army conducted surgical strikes on various terrorist launch pads across the Line of Control. These attacks were based on specific and credible inputs, and inflicted significant casualties to terrorists and those providing support to them.[5] The manner in which the attempts of Sri Ajit Doval, the Indian National Security Advisor, fell flat on their face after the meeting and parleys in Una reflects the treacherous and unreliable nature of Pakistan's establishment. Strangely, the Islamic Republic of Pakistan has never lamented and regretted or accepted its sponsorship, aiding and abating of cross-border terrorism which has been the key pin prick in the bilateral trade-offs between New Delhi and Islamabad.

The Mumbai terror attacks are a case in point about which Sunil Khilnani, the noted sociologist and anthropologist, writes, "That eve, I was taking a walk at the Gateway of India, and the Queen's Necklace, when the sirens, cries and splashes of the waves on the seafront were drowned by the sight of armed personnel guarding the yellow barricade by Nariman Point and the Gateway of India".[6] In a heinous and despicable act of cross-border terrorism on a convoy of Indian security forces in Pulwama, Jammu & Kashmir, on 14 February 2019, 40 security personnel were martyred. This terrorist act was perpetrated by the Jaish-e-Mohammed (JeM), a Pakistan-based and supported terrorist organisation proscribed by the United Nations and other countries. The organisation is led by the UN designated and internationally proscribed terrorist, Masood Azhar.

Thus, it can be conveniently surmised that numerous overtures for curbing terrorism of the cross-border variant along with the theme of fighting poverty jointly have been proposed and diplomatically ushered in by New Delhi. But instead of embarking on dialogue and a diplomatic pathway, the deep state of Pakistan has responded in a knee-jerk manner with astute, relative terror acts and subversion in the Indian homeland.

The Economist writes, "In the build-up to India's World Cup clash with Pakistan in Ahmedabad on 14 October, Indian news anchors spoke of 'the greatest rivalry'. For once, they were not exaggerating. Cricket contests between the South Asian giants have been their main interaction off the battlefield for three-quarters of a century. In them, each has poured subcontinental volumes of love and hate, nationalist chest-beating, an aching for peace, addiction to the fray, and the wholehearted commitment of two great and fascinatingly contrasting cricket cultures. Even for cricket ignoramuses, India-Pakistan bouts are an essential window into South Asian politics and culture. What, then, to make of the Ahmedabad match, which was attended by Banyan and ended in an easy Indian victory?"[7] Cricket nationalism has emerged as a guiding beacon of the entirety of the relationship between Islamabad and New Delhi. Who can forget the last ball six of Javed Miandad in Sharjah on the bowling of Chetan Sharma? In the same way, one still cherishes the incident in the World Cup match of 1996. Sohail Khan stroked a delivery by Venkatesh Prasad and pointed to the Indian bowler towards the square-off boundary line where the four had been hit. Venkatesh Prasad would have none of it as he bowled an unplayable off-cutter and the Paki willow-wielder nicked miserably to Indian wicket keeper Kiran More. The core message is that the angst, distrust and mutual acrimony manifests itself inside the cricket stadium and sheds useful light on the tardy state of affairs betwixt the India and Pakistan bilaterals.

The Economist further posits in the paper detailing the role of cricket as an adhesive between the twin nations. It enumerates, "Mostly the rivalry has become extremely lopsided, in cricket as in otherwise. India's win was its eighth on the trot over Pakistan in World Cups. And it was significantly crushing. The contest was held in the recently opened Narendra Modi Cricket Stadium, the cricket world's biggest, and attended by over 100,000 raucously partisan Indian fans."[8] Thus, both the nations have cricket-crazy fans, supporters and the entire narrative of the Paki defeats in the battlefields is recreated in the manner in which India has always trounced Pakistan on the cricket field. This is an instance out of the rule book of the enterprise of cricket nationalism.

The concept of the two-nation theory was widely accepted by Lord Mountbatten who was also called as 'Dickie'.[9] Mahatma Gandhi and Jawaharlal Nehru always supported the clarion call of a *Brahattar Bharat* which talked about a larger India spanning across the firmament of the Indian subcontinent. It was Mohammad Ali Jinnah of the Muslim League who came and initiated the tenet and concept of a separate nation of the Islamic Republic of Pakistan.

Pundit Nehru has gone ahead to contend upon the weak nature and intent of Pakistan during one of his utterances premised on Pakistan's weak state of domesticity. He said, "Pakistan...is developing today as an Islamic, feudal state. It is backward, reactionary, economically weak, administratively disrupted. The army is led by British officers. If they left there would be no Pakistani army Pakistan is a mediaeval state with an impossible theocratic concept. It should never have been created, and it would never have happened had the British not stood behind this foolish idea of Jinnah."[10]

A typical Indian statement on the whole question was the one made by the Prime Minister in Parliament on 17 May 1950: "It would be false and indeed inhuman of us to forget these friends who stood side by side with us for a whole generation in the fight for India's freedom. We are therefore intimately interested but it is a matter of abiding regret to us that *we can only* be *interested from* a *distance without being able to help in any way"*. It is also interesting that, unlike Khrushchev, Nehru never referred to the Pakhtoon problem in his public speeches during his visit to Afghanistan. In I96I, the validity of the Durand Line was accepted by the Indian Prime Minister.[11] Nehru had a liberal attitude towards Pakistan even after the Kabailee incursion over Srinagar and the larger neighbourhood province of Jammu and Kashmir. It was he who erroneously internationalised the border fracas and the confrontation over Kashmir by taking the matter to the United Nations. Repeated investigating teams have then gone ahead and recommended a plebiscite in the state of Jammu and Kashmir as a policy of solving the problem of Pakistan's erroneous claim over the state of Kashmir.

Pundit Jawaharlal Nehru during one of his speeches contended that "India and Pakistan being immediate neighbours can be the best of friends or can be hostile to each other. Both the neighbours can be friendly and compatible to each other despite the idea of the Partition. Pakistan's position is very peculiar in the manner in which Pakistan was formed and India was divided. The Government's decision in regard to the payment of the cash balances to Pakistan has been taken after the most careful thought and after consultation with Gandhiji. I should like to make it clear that this does not mean any change in our unanimous view about the strength and validity of the Government's position as set out in various statements made by distinguished colleagues of mine."[12]

While the present dispensation of Prime Minister Narendra Modi calls the spade a spade and has consistently stuck to a policy of explicating upon conditionality. As an attendant fact, it can be argued that the Pakistan-sponsored attacks at Uri, Balakot and Pathankot have served to smear the bilateral relationship between New Delhi and Islamabad into further discoloration. The present New Delhi dispensation views the normalcy of India-Pak relations as a theme which is inextricably enshrined within the theme of cross-border terrorism.

Prime Minister Narendra Modi, steeped in Indian culture and tradition, has, been a person with a core belief that India needs to attach the utmost strategic primacy to the nom de plume of a friendly and non-hostile neighbourhood. This facet was amply reflected in his invitation to all the heads of state of the South Asian neighbourhood in the May, 2014 inauguration of the Indian Government.

Rahul Roy Chaudhary writes, "Narendra Modi's government has placed India's neighbourhood as its top foreign policy priority. Modi's first official foreign trip was to neighbouring Bhutan. In just over a year he visited all of India's immediate neighbours, with the exception of Pakistan and the Maldives (where a planned visit was suddenly cancelled due to political differences). In an unprecedented move, he invited the seven other leaders in the South Asia Association for Regional Cooperation (SAARC), along with Mauritius, to his swearing-in ceremony in May 2014, holding his first set of meetings with them – including Pakistani Prime Minister Nawaz Sharif – the following day. He visited Pakistan in late 2016 for the SAARC summit, which was the first Indian prime ministerial visit to the country in over a decade."[13]

The European Council on Foreign Relations contends pithily, "Since independence nearly 70 years ago, India and Pakistan have fought three wars over Kashmir and one over Bangladesh. Once both acquired nuclear weapons in 1998, these shifted to lower-intensity military confrontations. Modi inherited difficult relations with Pakistan, after bilateral peace talks were suspended by his predecessor due to a spurt in violence and firing by Pakistan across the Line of Control (LoC) dividing the disputed Kashmir region."[14]

The European Council on Foreign Relations further reports, "Modi has hardened India's position towards Pakistan. He cancelled scheduled foreign-secretary level talks in August 2014 over a meeting between the Pakistani high commissioner to India and the Kashmiri separatist Hurriyat group. There was a distinct chill between Modi and Sharif at the SAARC summit in Kathmandu in November 2014. Then, in August 2015, India made it clear that it would not be acceptable for the visiting Pakistani national security advisor to meet the Hurriyat leadership or discuss anything other than terrorism, leading to the cancellation of scheduled talks between the two countries' national security advisors hours before they were to begin. India also deliberately intensified its firing across the LoC and the international border."[15] Earlier, it used to be a tradition amongst the UPA I and II regimes that track II diplomacy used to be adhered to by Pakistan's visiting dignitaries and diplomacy with India and Kashmir-based separatist leaders. This diplomatic trend was a major cause of concern amongst the Indian hoi polloi along with the dedicated nationalist citizens of the Bharatiya nation. But since the advent of the nationalist Bharatiya Janata Party, it has become the order of the day that New Delhi has disallowed the holding of talks between visiting Pakistani diplomatic delegations with the separatist leaders of the state of Kashmir which has rankled nerves in the Pakistani establishment. This hardened tenor of Prime Minister Narendra Modi happens to be the key characteristic and hallmark of the larger policy of Bharat towards the intransigence and the non-cooperation dished out to New Delhi in the contemporary past.

"Two years after Narendra Modi became prime minister of India, how should we understand his foreign policy? Commentators are divided on whether or not Modi has brought anything new to it. The highly respected former diplomat and Foreign Secretary, Shyam Saran, argues that Modi's external policies have built on the past; that the difference between Modi and his predecessors is a matter of energy and style. By contrast, a leading Indian commentator, C. Raja Mohan, regards Modi's rule as presaging the start of a 'Third Republic' and a new foreign policy."[16] Thus, PM Modi has ushered in a more muscular, aggressive and proacative policy to the fore as far as relations and transactions with the Islamic Republic of Pakistan are concerned. He has been adhering to a policy of tit for tat in accordance with the IR games and thus has brought in a much needed intent in Indian foreign policy and diplomacy with Pakistan.

Kanti Vajpai further writes, "Modi's China policy, like his Pakistan policy, is clear and consistent. He has emphasized the need to resolve the border problem and other differences if the overall relationship is to progress, thus reversing the approach adhered to by New Delhi since 1988. He has engaged with the Chinese leadership but has departed from conventional summitry with some assertive bilateral diplomacy and active coalition diplomacy before and after the summits. More so than with Pakistan, Modi is attempting to construct a coalition to strengthen India's bargaining hand and, in the case of the Indian Ocean states, its maritime security."[17]

It can be argued that PM Modi's strivings to spawn a coalition to surround and contain China and Pakistan has become the order, especially in the light of the Indian overtures in the oceanic space and the Asia Pacific theatre. India under Modi aims to contain Pakistan though it is a completely different matter that Pakistan's disaster wheeling and dealing with the Border Road Initiative of China along with its recent economic crisis have further bedevilled the domestic scenario in a beleaguered and unstable Islamic Republic of Pakistan. This can be gleaned from the recent Indian overtures in the context in the QUAD grouping of nations along with the larger idiom of strangulating Pakistan and China as is evident in the efforts to strengthen defence and security cooperation with nations of the order of Australia. It has been written, "Modi's trip to Australia in November 2014, the first by an Indian prime minister in 28 years, signalled a clear change. His address to the Australian parliament – the first ever by an Indian prime minister – was enthusiastically received. He got on well personally with Prime Minister

Tony Abbott. Most importantly, the two sides agreed on a framework for security cooperation that provides for annual dialogues between the respective prime ministers, foreign ministers and defence ministers."[18]

It is further informed, "To get Pakistan to change its approach to terrorism, New Delhi has 'defected' from talks and negotiations when Islamabad has forced the Kashmir issue. Also, when there have been terrorist strikes and surges in cross-border artillery fire towards India has been diplomatically discomfited. For the longer term, Modi is attempting to build an international coalition including key Gulf countries. This development will bring pressures to bear on Islamabad to rein in terrorist activities from its soil and to bring to book those involved in organizing cross-border attacks. Modi's approach has departed from India's Pakistan policy 'script' in two ways. He has sought to change the terms of engagement by focusing on terrorism to the exclusion of the Kashmir dispute; and he has gone beyond India's insistence on bilateralism in dispute resolution by embracing a coalition strategy."[19]

An alternate approach by left and liberal thinkers, academics and foreign policy observers happens to be that of an engineered benign and peaceful South Asia. A consideration of New Delhi and Islamabad working as collaborates in cooperative sync with each other may appear too superfluous and inane and impractical., Some observers posing to be avant garde tend to bring in the analogy of China and India co-existing in the face of 'Chindia' wherein India and Pakistan too can be made to eschew their mammoth differences and confrontations, both ideologically and practically.

When one talks about soft power, then sports and more particularly cricket, can be the order of the day in which the two cricket teams of India and Pakistan envision a social and softly sporty understanding and comprehension between the cricket crazy populations of both the nations. To reiterate, Bharat and Pakistan are the greatest rivals on and off the cricketing pitch populated by the willow wielders and the wicket guzzlers. The story of India and Pakistani cricket relations is not a bilateral one but a triangular one. It involves not only the cricketers and administrators of the two countries but also India's huge Muslim population. Their position, and in particular what the majority Hindu community perceives to be their attitude, is part of this story.

When the Pakistani dictator, General Pervez Musharraf, complimented the Indian star on the rise, Mahendra Singh Dhoni, he also commented on his wild and novae hair styles with hair dangling all over his shoulders and neck. Thus, cricket diplomacy happens to be the order of day whenever an Indian team visits Pakistan or a Paki team comes to play matches in Bharat. One can cite some monumental moments of India-Pakistan cricket rivalry both on and off the field.

Mihir Bose writes in a Warwick University release, "The first Test at Chennai saw Pakistan set India a target of 273. The match looked all over at 82 for 5 but among the unbeaten five was Tendulkar. His 136 nearly brought victory, India failing by 12 runs. The second Test at Kotla not only brought India victory but made history. Pakistan, set 419, had made a good start, getting to 101 for no loss at lunch on the fourth day. But after lunch, the Indian spin bowler Anil Kumble changed ends, from the football stand end to the pavilion end. In nineteen overs and three balls he took all ten wickets, only the second time since Jim Laker (against Australia in 1956) that a Test bowler had done so. Although this marked the end of the two-Test series, India and Pakistan played a third match in what was billed as the Asian Test championship. This match showed the destructive passions India–Pakistan cricket can generate. India, after making a great start by reducing Pakistan to 26 for 6 on the first day, had a fight on its hands, being set 278 to win in their second innings."[20]

Mihir Bose further writes, "How explosive this fight could be was soon demonstrated. There occurred two incidents which ignited the Kolkata crowd and shamed Indian cricket. Tendulkar, on 9, hit a ball to the boundary and in going for a third – his second had taken him past 5,000 Test runs – he collided with Pakistan's Shoaib Akhtar at the bowler's end and was run out. The crowd felt Akhtar had deliberately blocked him and forced the game to come to a stop. Tendulkar and Dalmiya, the ICC President, had to appeal to them before play could resume."[21] The author further asserts, "But the crowd was on edge and on the final morning, when their hero Sourav Ganguly failed and with India facing certain defeat on 251 for 9, they rioted. The police evicted all the spectators and, with only about 200 VIPs, officials and journalists present, Pakistan won by 26 runs. After Kumble's deeds at Delhi, the behaviour of the fans and the incompetence of the authorities represented a sad and dishonourable episode for Indian cricket. The defeat also meant that in effect two successive Pakistani visits to India had resulted in their going home victors. But the tide was about to turn for India and it was Ganguly, the man at the centre of the drama in Kolkata, who engineered it."[22]

Only the militaries have sagely witnessed and waged war against Pakistan's forces in 1947, 1965, 1971, 1999 and 2019, but both the nations came close to war once the two teams of the cricketing nations play out a daredevil and crucially winsome battle of the willow and the ball at the stadium are must not forget Uri and Balakot. The mass frenzy and the media extravaganza are inbuilt parts of the entire circus. The warring heroes and icons all the way from Sourav Ganguly, Sachin Tendulkar and Virendra Sehwag to Viral Kohli and the present-day Indian skipper, Rohit Sharma, disembark from the pavilions to disembowel the enemy which is another take on the rival Pakistan's cricketing team.

Apart from cricket rivalry and the idiom of cricket nationalism, one can focus upon the theme of the 'failed nation concept; which the larger ilk of international relations and observers of the political economy have seemed to festoon upon the Pakistan. The Pakistani national daily, *Dawn,* posed a poser in August 2023 why is Pakistan failing as a nation in the context of the economic crisis in the nation. The political instability and political violence was ushered in by the imprisonment and impeachment of the iconic Pakistani Premier, Imran Khan, in the recent past. *Dawn* reported, "These disclosures by the former FBR chief show the power of a rent-seeking ruling elite. It shows that the country's entire power structure is built to serve the corporate interests of powerful ruling classes, both civil and military."[23]

The newspaper further reports, "It was revealing how the then army chief intervened to block adjustment of property valuation in the Defence Housing Authority by the FBR as it affected the property business in the vicinity controlled by military authorities. It was apparently meant to protect the security establishment's expanding corporate interests. Trading in property allotted to military officers has become a lucrative business. Perks come with the power that the establishment wields. There is certainly no check on its power. It should, then, really not come as a surprise that while burdening the masses with more taxes, as part of the IMF's programme, the finance minister has refrained from broadening the tax net to real estate, retail business and big landlords. It is basically corporate interests that determine our financial policy priorities. The weakening of state institutions has prevented the country from embarking on the path of economic progress and ending financial dependence on multilateral agencies and external donors. The failure to broaden the tax base is a manifestation of the continued stranglehold of a small narrow elite. This facet has left the state with few resources for the development of economic infrastructure. It also makes the country more dependent on foreign aid. Tax revenue as a percentage of GDP has stagnated at 10 per cent over the last decade and has been declining. It is shocking that the taxes paid by National Assembly lawmakers fail to match their lifestyle. The FBR has failed to take action despite this fact."[24]

According to data compiled by the FBR, the salaried classes pay 200 per cent more taxes than the combined taxes paid by the country's exporters and highly under-taxed retailers. While more taxes have been piled on the salaried classes in the last budget, thousands of retailers have conveniently been left out of the tax net because of political reasons. How strong the business lobbies are was witnessed last year when a tweet from Maryam Nawaz forced the then finance minister, Miftah Ismail, to withdraw even a nominal tax on retailers. It was unprecedented that a budgetary provision passed by parliament was arbitrarily withdrawn following a tweet from a leader of the main ruling party.

The control of a narrow oligarchic elite over our political system has impeded the implementation of structural reforms that are critical to sustainable economic development and are required for strengthening economic and other institutions. In nearly 76 years of independence, democratically elected governments have been mere punctuation marks in a long reign of military and autocratic political rule.

Unfortunately, there has been no fundamental change in Pakistan's political power structure during that period. A small power elite has dominated Pakistan's political scene under both civilian and military rule. For too long, the country has traded on the back of its strategic resources and geopolitical importance, making its rulers totally dependent on international financial aid. It is not only about reliance on external aid but also about an economy based on internal rents limiting our productive capacity.

Thus, the entire discussion about Pakistan either being a failed state or a decidedly and apparently failing nation unfortunately posits a very grim and existential question towards the political leadership of the country. Declaring the Islamic Republic of Pakistan as a failed state and not a 'failing nation' can be a dangerous proposition but still what cannot escape our notice is the theme that Pakistan, akin to Sri Lanka, finds itself in the lurch geo- economically. It can be attributed to the China-sponsored Border Road Initiative which has wedged into Pakistan's economy and largely stalled the real-time development parameters of the besieged and beleaguered nation.

Subhash Kapila writes in the journal of the Institute of Peace and Conflict Studies, "Political theorists would keep splitting hairs as to what factors really constitute a failing state. Conventional wisdom would have it that a state, which is unable to guard democracy and its political institutions, whose economy has failed.[25] A state that lacks social development and is plagued by sectarian strife is heading towards a failed state status." Thus, the misery and the vulnerability of Pakistan as a stolid and well-performing nation in the realm of domestic governance is at stake. Also this attracts cagey appellations of the order of a 'Failed/Failing state'. Subhash Kapila further writes, "After 52 years of independence, both civil and military rulers of Pakistan have been unable to put Pakistan's economy on a stable footing despite having rich resources of energy and inheriting the best irrigated portions of British India and a small population to sustain."[26]

The economic picture today is dismal with a foreign debt of over $ 30 billion, foreign currency reserves less than $ 1 billion alongside IMF's refusal to release $ 280 million of a $ 1.6 billion aid package. The core reasons for Pakistan's failing economy are its heavy defence expenditure in a bid to reach symmetry with India and rampant corruption of Pakistan's civil and military rulers."[27]

The fien the siècle is provided by the author when he writes about the divergence of sectarianism and fissiparous regional divides in the Pakistani polity. The author says, "The common saying is 'Pakistan is Punjab and Punjab is Pakistan." The Punjabi dominance in Pakistan's power elite fosters provincial divisiveness and resentment of Punjabi control on the levers of power. Despite being a theocratic Islamic state, Islam has not been able to bind the various provinces of Pakistan (ethnically different) nor prevent violent sectarian strife between the two major sects of Islam – Sunnis and Shias. The social structures in Pakistan remain feudal and exploitative. Budgetary allocations for social developments especially education and health are dismal, due to heavy expenditure on defence."[28] When for instance one talks about Pakistan's political and military elites, then one can conveniently zero in upon the notion why Nawaz Sharif is planning to return to Pakistan's political firmament and pose himself as a prime ministerial option in the light of an imprisoned Imran Khan. As is rightly pointed out, the centrality of the money and muscle power of the province of Punjab has been found too powerful and influential for the madrasas. too.

In the context of the central thrust of India's foreign policy, New Delhi has always maintained that Kashmir is an integral part and parcel of the Bharatiya ethos and existence. The nation is not prepared to compromise on its foundational edifice of territorial integrity and centrality of its narrative of nationhood. *The Statesman* reports, "The regime is proud of unveiling the Jammu and Kashmir Reorganization and Reservation Act's amendments, wherein the Government showcases that since the abrogation of Article 370, the entire state of Jammu and

Kashmir has witnessed a fall in the terror incidents in the beleaguered valley to an appreciable 70 per cent. There has been no incident of stone pelting since the 2022 and along with these positive developments, there have been only 48 incidents of infiltration along with two incidents of ceasefire violations."[29]

The New Delhi dispensation under Prime Minister Narendra Modi has consistently maintained that there happens to be an inviolable inseparability of the theme of Kashmir as far as New Delhi's external relations go. Since the internationalisation of the mandate of the province of Jammu and Kashmir, the mistake of agreeing to a third party-mediated plebiscite has been a cardinal mistake by the free Indian establishment. Since those halcyon days, the Paki strategic striving has been to propagandize against Bharat in myriad international fora and institutions which has to be answered by the Indian foreign policy establishment. Thus, Kashmir has served as an illegitimate stick and brickbat which the Paki nation has deftly utilised to paint New Delhi in the red as a human rights transgressor and suppressor of the imagined sovereignty of the Indian state.

For decades, India has tried to thwart Pakistan in a protracted dispute over Kashmir, the achingly beautiful Himalayan territory claimed by both countries but divided between them. That relentless competition always made Pakistan the focus of New Delhi's foreign policy. But in the last two years, since a deadly border clash between Indian and Chinese soldiers in Kashmir's Ladakh region, policymakers in New Delhi have been increasingly turning their focus towards Beijing, a significant shift in policy as the nation celebrates 75 years of independence.[30]

The portal *Diplomat* informs, "India's ever-growing economy, which is now vastly larger than Pakistan's, combined with Beijing's increasingly assertive push for influence across Asia, means that 'New Delhi has increasingly grown Beijing-centric,' said Lt. Gen. D.S. Hooda, who from 2014 to 2016 headed the Indian military's Northern Command which controls Kashmir, including Ladakh. Kashmir has suffered insurgencies, lockdowns and political subterfuge since India and Pakistan gained independence from British colonial rule in 1947, and has been at the heart of two of the four wars India has fought with Pakistan and China. The three countries' tense borders meet at the disputed territory in the world's only three-way nuclear confrontation."[31]

The *Diplomat* further informs, "Starting in the 1960s, India was an active member of the Non-Aligned Movement, a grouping of over 100 countries that theoretically did not align with any major power during the Cold War. Despite disputes with neighbouring Pakistan and China, India's nonaligned stance remained the bedrock of its foreign policy. Its diplomats focused mainly on upending Pakistan's claim to Kashmir. 'Kashmir was in a way central to our foreign policy concerns,' said Kanwal Sibal, a career diplomat who was India's foreign secretary in 2002-2003. But, the current military standoff between India and China over their disputed border in Ladakh set off a grave escalation in tensions between the two Asian giants. Despite 17 rounds of diplomatic and military talks, the tense standoff continues. For decades, India believed China did not represent a military threat, said Hooda, the former military commander."[32]

The portal informs pithily, "But that calculus changed in mid-2020 when a clash high in the Karakoram mountains in Ladakh's Galwan Valley set off military tensions. 'Galwan represents a strategic inflection point,' said Constantino Xavier, a fellow at the Centre for Social and Economic Progress. It helped create a new Indian consensus about the need to reset the entire relationship with China, and not just solve the boundary issue."[33] Thus, a poser might be raised here about the urgent and ultra significance being accorded to the Chinese threat. In a manner, the Pakistan's military threat has ceased to exist since the occurrence of the natural disaster in the form of the excessive flooding of the antagonist nation and then the engulfment of Pakistan by the Chinese triggered and the IMF and WB exacerbated task. The nation is in immense debt though it ought not to be forgotten that other nations such as Greece in 2016 and Sri Lanka in the recent past have faced similar strafing scenarios. These debilitating circumstances economically brought about their hoi polloi to a miserable and gruesome state of affairs. Even the

United States of America in recent years has witnessed Congressional duels in order to mitigate the exacerbation of the debt ceiling crisis. In the USA, the White House has been forced to borrow to prevent the national economy from collapsing and keep running the regular flow of wages of government employees.

The Water Wars

It has been observed by international relations scholars and others of every ilk that the wars being fought in the future will be rooted in the allocation of natural resources such as water, oil, food and energy. Within the context of India-Pakistan wars, it can be surmised that the division and overall flow of the Indus River and its system of tributaries needs to be studied and zeroed in upon. Both the nations have been at loggerheads concerning the project of the Baglihar Dam.

The water power and dam construction portal contends, "India had decided to set up a run-of-river, 450 MW hydroelectric plant at Baglihar in its Jammu & Kashmir State, utilizing the waters of the Chenab River, a tributary of the mighty Indus. Since the time that India informed Pakistan of that fact in 1992, the two countries had gone through prolonged negotiations based on Pakistan's objections to the project as the lower riparian state. The talks, not having succeeded, a World Bank – appointed 'neutral' expert is currently engaged in the task of finding a solution."[34]

The portal further informs, "To understand the imbroglio, it is necessary to look at the bigger picture. The Indus river system, one of the major systems in the world, comprises the main Indus and its five important tributaries: Jhelum, Chenab, Ravi, Beas and Sutlej rivers. For the sake of convenience and geography, the Indus, along with Jhelum and Chenab, are referred to as the 'western rivers', while the other three tributaries are termed as 'eastern rivers'. The common features of all of them is that they originate in the Himalayas, pass through Indian territory and, after Indus has received the waters of its five tributaries in Pakistan, it flows through the Pak provinces of Punjab and Sind and fall in the Arabian Sea, south of Karachi.

After the British had colonised India in the 19th century, they built a large network of dams, barrages and canals over eight decades utilizing the Indus river system. The command area so created of about 105 mha was the largest such irrigated tract in the world and turned the Indian province of Punjab (literally meaning 'Five Waters') and its contiguous areas from a mainly arid zone into a prosperous agrarian state that grew both food grains and cash crops.

The portal further informs, "Britain granted independence to India in 1947 by partitioning the sub-continent into two separate political entities of India and Pakistan. The process of partition (and its aftermath in Kashmir) led to an arbitrary split of the Indus river system, with its parts divided between the two countries. The river's sources and headworks of some major canals remained in India. The latter drew plans to further develop the water resources which remained on its side. Pakistan, as the smaller state, located downstream of these rivers, felt threatened that India could well manipulate the flow of those waters to the former's disadvantage."[35]

Still, one may cite the argument that Pakistan ceases to be a military threat to India in the light of the floods and the near to strafing run of the economic collapse in Pakistan. David Brewster writes in the eminent of the Lowy Institute, "Pakistan is undergoing a protracted political and economic crisis, putting it on track to become a significant problem for the Indo-Pacific region. The country's political instability and prospects of economic default are likely to have far-reaching consequences, including in Pakistan's standoff with India and its role as China's regional proxy. Pakistan's current political upheaval not only threatens the government under Prime Minister Shehbaz Sharif, but also the army's role in Pakistan's politics. At the same time, years of economic mismanagement are coming home to roost. Pakistan now finds itself unable to repay loans used to fund deficits and wasteful and corrupt projects, including through the China–Pakistan Economic Corridor (CPEC)."[36]

The Lowy Institute journal writes, "Washington has little interest in bailing Islamabad (and its Chinese creditors) out of the hole that it has dug for itself. A default on Pakistan's external debts, which stood at US$ 126 billion as at the end of 2022, now seems increasingly likely. Many believe that Pakistan can avoid a debt default this month only with the release of another tranche of IMF funds. Multinational companies are exiting the country, while Pakistan International Airlines aircraft are being seized by creditors. Large numbers of Pakistanis, many of them educated middle-class, are leaving to find better futures, including some 800,000 people in 2022. These departures will increasingly involve more desperate means – as shown by the more than 300 Pakistanis who died in the recent refugee boat disaster off Greece. Australia, too, may see a surge in arrivals from Pakistan."[37] It has been depicted and portrayed by the international media that Pakistan's work force even from the rather stable and stolid government sector went to Egypt in flights and went to Libya and from there on boarded unsafe and hazardous boats to Greece illegally and illegitimately in order to initiate a new earning and attain a peaceful and assured lifestyle away from the dismembered and torn context of their homeland, that is, the Islamic Republic of Pakistan.

David Brewster further writes, "Unfortunately, Pakistan has an ever-decreasing number of friends to help it out of the crisis. Washington has little interest in bailing Islamabad (and its Chinese creditors) out of the hole that it has dug for itself. Pakistan's role in the fall of Kabul is well remembered and US aid has slowed to a trickle. Even Islamabad's Middle Eastern partners are losing interest. Traditional backers such as Saudi Arabia, the United Arab Emirates and Qatar are reportedly reluctant to provide further bailouts. In February, in what was seen as a slap in the face, Türkiye's President Recep Tayyip Erdogan used Twitter to cancel a planned visit by Prime Minister Shehbaz."[38]

Earlier, Pakistan used to be a frontline state for Washington, wherein, American designs against the Cold War rival, the Soviet Union, were undertaken unhesitatingly and overtly by Pakistan's regime of General Zia-ul-Haq. Other nations such as the quintessential supporters and succour providers such as the United Arab Emirates and Saudi Arabia too have backed off from extricating Islamabad from the mess it finds itself in the aftermath of the economic crisis.

Still, if we delve into the military comparisons of New Delhi and Rawalpindi then we have causes of worry as Pakistan happens to own a lean and ill-meaning machine of adversarial warfare and where, though India has turned Beijing-centric in its military and defence approach, the Pakistan threat still cannot be downplayed keeping in view the stolid stealth of the deep state in our adversary nation, that is, the Islamic Republic of Pakistan.

Let us delve into the budgetary part of the comparisons between India and Pakistan. *Al Jazeera* reports, "In 2018, India allocated four trillion rupees ($ 58 bn), or 2.1 per cent of its gross domestic product (GDP), to support its 1.4 million active troops, according to the International Institute for Strategic Studies (IISS). Last year, Pakistan spent 1.26 trillion Pakistani rupees ($ 11 bn), about 3.6 per cent of its GDP, on its 653,800 troops. It also received $ 100 m in foreign military assistance in 2018. Between 1993 and 2006, more than 20 per cent of Pakistan's annual government expenditure was spent on the military, according to estimates from the Stockholm International Peace Research Institute (SIPRI)."[39] Thus, it can be safely surmised that New Delhi can well afford to augment the defence budget in order to meet up Pakistan's challenge. Prime Minister Narendra Modi has ably chaperoned the increment in the Indian military budget over the last few years. This meets with the modernization and acquisition challenges of the Indian armed forces.

The wars earlier used to be fought between nations for territory and prestige but since the last few decades the theme of resource allocation happens to be the order of the day. For instance, the division and sharing of the waters of the Indus River leading to the threat that in the case of a war the entire Pakistan, being a lower riparian state, will be flooded by India by opening up its water barrages and dams. This leads to a disruption of Pakistan's life and the war prospects of the country. Also, wars used to be quick and swift but now the Ukraine-Russia conflict has taught us that wars are strife prone, replete with attrition along with being long dragging. A great stretch on the economies of the adversaries is a gruesome burden for the global economy.

One can delve inside the raison d'etre of the Indus water treaty. Herein, the original and classical understanding of the Indus River system lies. The Ministry of Jal Shakti states, "At the time of independence, the boundary line between the two newly-created independent countries, i.e., Pakistan and India, was drawn right across the Indus Basin, leaving Pakistan as the lower riparian. Moreover, two important irrigation head works, one at Madhopur on the Ravi River and the other at Ferozepur on the Sutlej River, on which the irrigation canal supplies in Punjab (Pakistan) had been completely dependent, were left in Indian territory. A dispute thus arose between two countries regarding the utilization of irrigation water from existing facilities. Negotiations held under the good offices of the International Bank for Reconstruction and Development (World Bank) that culminated in the signing of the Indus Waters Treaty in 1960. The Treaty was signed at Karachi by Field Marshal Mohammad Ayub Khan, the then President of Pakistan, Shri Jawaharlal Nehru, the then Indian Prime Minister and Mr. W.A.B. Illif of the World Bank on 19 September 1960. The Treaty however is effective from1 April, 1960."[40] Despite the two neighbours having agreed on paper upon the fundamentals of water sharing, the nation-state of Pakistan raises a great deal of hue and cry over the wartime fallouts of the Indus water treaty and further water sharing arrangements."

The Ministry of External Affairs states, "*Article II of the Indus water treaty grants unlimited rights to the Indian Union to utilise and divert the Indus river water for its national consumption and themes such as the points of crossing, the extent of use and utilisation by India are well entrenched in the text of the Treaty. The Treaty also clearly mentions the nature and extent of water usage by Pakistan in the text which originally did not have any iota of fracas with the either nation's riparian rights.*"

The text of the Treaty can be reproduced here which posits the exact conditionality along with the riparian rights of the both the nations.

"Provisions Regarding Eastern Rivers

1. All the waters of the Eastern Rivers shall be available for the

unrestricted use of India, except as otherwise expressly provided in this Article.

2. Except for Domestic Use and Non-Consumptive Use, Pakistan shall be under an obligation to let flow, and shall not permit any interference with, the waters of the Sutlej Main and the Ravi Main in the reaches where these rivers flow in Pakistan and have not yet finally crossed into Pakistan. The Points of final crossing are the following: (a) near the new Hasta Bund upstream of Suleimanke in the case of the Sutlej Main, and (b) about one and a half miles upstream of the siphon for the B-R-B-D Link in the case of the Ravi Main.
3. Except for Domestic Use, Non-Consumptive Use and Agricultural Use (as specified in Annexure B), Pakistan shall be under an obligation to let flow, and shall not permit any interference with, the waters (while flowing in Pakistan) of any Tributary which in its natural course joins the Sutlej Main or the Ravi Main before these rivers have finally crossed into Pakistan.[41]
4. All the waters, while flowing in Pakistan, of any Tributary which, in its natural course, joins the Sutlej Main or the Ravi Main after these rivers have finally crossed into Pakistan shall be available for the unrestricted use of Pakistan: Provided however that this provision shall not be construed as giving Pakistan any claim or right to any releases by India in any such Tributary. If Pakistan should deliver any of the waters of any such Tributary, which on the Effective Date joins the Ravi Main after this river has finally crossed into Pakistan, into a reach of the Ravi Main upstream of this crossing, India shall not make use of these waters; each Party agrees to establish such discharge observation stations and make such observations as may be necessary for the determination of the component of water available[42] for the use of Pakistan on account of the aforesaid deliveries by Pakistan, and Pakistan agrees to meet the cost of establishing the aforesaid discharge observation stations and making the aforesaid observations.

5. There shall be a Transition Period during which, to the extent specified in Annexure H, India shall

    I. limit its withdrawals for Agricultural Use,

    II. limit abstractions for storages, and

    III. make deliveries to Pakistan from the Eastern Rivers.

6. The Transition Period shall begin on 1st April 1960 and it shall end on 31st March 1970, or, if extended under the provisions of Part 8 of Annexure H, on the date up to which it has been extended. In any event, whether or not the replacement referred to in Article IV(1) has been accomplished, the Transition Period shall end not later than 31st March 1973.

7. If the Transition Period is extended beyond 31st March 1970, the Provisions of Article V(5) shall apply.

8. If the Transition Period is extended beyond 31st March 1970, the provisions of Paragraph (5) shall apply during the period of extension beyond 31st March 1970.

9. During the Transition Period, Pakistan shall receive for unrestricted use the waters of the Eastern Rivers which are to be released by India in accordance with the provisions of Annexure H. After the end of the Transition Period, Pakistan shall have no claim or right to releases by India of any of the waters of the Eastern Rivers. In case there are any releases, Pakistan shall enjoy the unrestricted use of the waters so released after they have finally crossed into Pakistan: Provided that in the event that Pakistan makes any use of these waters, Pakistan shall not acquire any right whatsoever, by prescription or otherwise, to a continuance of such releases or such use.

Article III

Provisions Regarding Western Rivers

1. Pakistan shall receive for unrestricted use all those waters of the Western Rivers which India is under obligation to let flow under the provisions of Paragraph (2).

2. India shall be under an obligation to let flow all the waters of the Western Rivers, and shall not permit any interference with these waters, except for the following uses, restricted (except as provided in item (c) (11) of Paragraph 5 of Annexure C) in the case of each of the rivers, The Indus, the Jhelum and the Chenab, to the drainage basin thereof

   I. Domestic Use:

   II. Non-Consumptive Use;

   III. Agricultural Use, as set out in Annexure C; and

   IV. Generation of hydro-electric power, as set out in Annexure D.

3. Pakistan shall have the unrestricted use of all waters originating from sources other than the Eastern Rivers which are delivered by Pakistan into the Ravi or the Sutlej, and India shall not make use of these waters. Each Party agrees to establish such discharge observation stations and make such observations as may be considered necessary by the Commission for the determination of the component of water available for the use of Pakistan on account of the aforesaid deliveries by Pakistan.

4. Except as provided in Annexures D and E, India shall not store any water of, or construct any storage works on, the Western Rivers.[43]

Another theme which appears contentious from Pakistan's point of view is that of the transition period. The transition period is defined as the next eleven years from 1960 wherein India after 1971 will be asked to delimit its usage and attendant utilization of the Indus River water which will be constrained keeping in view the interests of the lower riparian state which Pakistan is. This has been spiced up and propagandized by Pakistan in order to besmirch the Indian case and official standpoint. Also, the treaty makes it very clear that Pakistan too can make individual unhindered utilization of the rivers of the order of Sutlej and Ravi but has no rights whatsoever over the waters of the eastern rivers. It's here that the Modi dispensation has contended that Pakistan has a dedicatedly designated share of water and it has been incorrectly alleging and accusing New Delhi that India makes excessive usage of the water in the eastern rivers which are not all marked for utilization by the Pakistan's establishment and its related popular interests.

NOTES

1. 'Bilateral Brief: India Pakistan Relations,' URL https://india.org.pk/pages.php?id=16 (Online Web), accessed on 10 October 2023.
2. Ibid.
3. Ibid 1., Fn. 1.
4. Ibid 2,. Fn. 2.
5. Ibid., Fn. 3.
6. Sunil Khilnani. '*The Idea of India*,' Penguin, New Delhi, 1996, pp. 1-10.
7. 'India Pakistan Relations are becoming more marginal and worse,' *The Economist*, October, 2023.
8. Ibid.
9. Stanley Walport. '*The India Pakistan Relations*', Penguin, India, 2011.
10. Joseph Korbel. '*Danger in Kashmir',* Princeton, NJ., I954,, pp. 128, 130.
11. *Asian Recorder,* New Delhi, vol. 7, p. 4250.
12. Jawaharlal Nehru's Speeches, September1946–May 1949, Government of India, Ministry of Information and Broadcasting, Publications Division, 1954, p. 296.
13. Rahul Roy Chaudhary. 'Modi's Approach to China and Pakistan,' URL https://ecfr.eu/special/what_does_india_think/analysis/modis_approach_to_india_and_pakistan (Online: Web), Accessed on 10 October 2023.
14. Ibid.
15. Ibid., Fn. 1.
16. Kanti Bajpai. "Narendra Modi's Pakistan and China Policy: Assertive Bilateral Diplomacy and Active, Coalition Diplomacy," URL https://www.chathamhouse.org/sites/default/files/publications/ia/INTA93_1_05_Bajpai.pdf (Online: Web), Accessed on 10 November 2023.
17. Ibid.
18. 'Framework for security cooperation between India and Australia', Narendra Modi website, 18 November 2014, http://www.narendramodi.in/framework-for-security-cooperation-between-india-and-australia-6907.
19. Ibid.
20. Mihir Bose. 'Conflicting loyalties: Nationalism and Religion in India-Pakistan cricket relations,' URL https://warwick.ac.uk/fac/arts/history/students/modules/hi2b6/programme/week3/conflicting_loyalties_nationalism_and_religion_in_indiapakistan_cricket_relations.pdf (Online Web), Accessed on 10 November 2023.
21. Ibid.
22. Ibid 1, Fn. 1.
23. Zahid Hussain. 'Why Pakistan is Failing,' *Dawn*, 2 August 2023.
24. Ibid.
25. Subhash Kapila. 'Pakistan: A Failing State,' URL http://www.ipcs.org/comm_select.php?articleNo=277 (Online: Web), accessed on 1 December 2023.
26. Ibid.

27. Ibid., Fn. 1.
28. Ibid., Fn. 2.
29. Correspondent. 'Amit Shah discusses J and K,' *The Statesman*, 7 December, 2023.
30. *The Diplomat*. URL https://thediplomat.com/2022/08/at-75-indias-kashmir-challenge-shifts-foreign-policy-focus/ (Online: Web), accessed on 28 November 2023.
31. Ibid.
32. Ibid.
33. Ibid.
34. 'The Baglihar Dispute', URL https://www.waterpowermagazine.com/news/newsthe-baglihar-dispute (Online: Web), accessed on 10 May 2023.
35. Ibid.
36. David Brewster. 'Why the Pakistan Crisis spells trouble for the Region,' URL https://www.lowyinstitute.org/the-interpreter/why-pakistan-crisis-spells-trouble-our-region (Online: Web), accessed on 10 December 2023.
37. Ibid.
38. Ibid 1
39. War Correspondent Desk, "India Vs Pakistan: Comparisons of Military Arsenals," URL: https://www.aljazeera.com/news/2019/2/26/india-vs-pakistan-military-strength-and-arsenal (Online: Web), Accessed on 10 November, 2023
40. "Indus Water Treaty 1960" URL: https://jalshakti-dowr.gov.in/indus-waters-treaty-1960/ (Online: Web), Accessed on May 10, 2023
41. "Ministry of External Affairs Release," URL: https://www.mea.gov.in/bilateral-documents.htm?dtl/6439/Indus (Online: Web), Accessed on November 10, 2023)
42. Ibid
43. Ibid., Fn. 1.

Chapter Four

India and China 'Bilaterals': The Strange Case of Recurrence and Repetitions

When one talks about the China-India bilateral relations, one can hardly emerge out of the pessimism of the 1962 military defeat when New Delhi was caught unawares by the border skirmish. Though the bone of contentions for the two antagonist nations are multifold, the idea of China being the epicentre of the COVID epidemic along with the economic rivalry with Beijing and the Chinese support to the arch enemy, Pakistan, too happen to be rankling elements between the two nations. Still, the border fracas between both the nations is the major cause of enquiry and diabolic narrative as hewn by the People's Republic of China. One may delve into the fundamentals of the India-China border conflict.

The single most significant irritant in India-China relations can be attributed to the India-China border dispute, which mars the good the India-China relations. The Indian approach has been to carry on with the trade and other diplomatic and political aspects of the relationship. It is a well-known fact that miles of border separate the two antagonist nations, which are recognised by the two countries, with the People's Republic of China refusing to agree to the McMahon Line demarcation between New Delhi and Beijing. The Chinese stand happens to be that the Chinese representative in the Simla conference in 1913 was not allowed entry into the room while the Chinese and the British delegates confabulated inside, without the Chinese diplomats. Thus, the Chinese diplomatic standpoint is that because of the non-participation of the Chinese side, the legal integrity of the McMahon Line as the LAC (Line of Actual Control) is tenacious.

The entire historicity of the border is contested by Beijing which culminated in the 1962 border war between the two nations. Also, the entire dispute amounts to a cartographic contestation by the Chinese as even after a meeting between Pundit Jawaharlal Nehru and Mao Tse Tung in 1952. Here in the Chinese published maps showing Arunachal Pradesh and Aksai Chin as Chinese territory. Through their contemporary policy and strategy of usurping Taiwan and the South China Sea Island, their claims are premised on the principles of sovereignty, rule of law and territorial integrity.

India dubs China's claims over the territory as part of Beijing's expansionist designs. The process of Chinese cartographic mapping until the 1970s reflects the singular cartographic claim of Beijing on Indian territory and land. The earliest interpretations, which were carried out in the decades of the 'Twenties and 'Thirties, reflected no Chinese assertions on India's territories. Still, these maps were very much divergent from the maps inherited from the times of the royal Manchu dynasty, along with any prevailing and extant maps of the 1920s and 1930s, which was portentous for the British colonial raj and the cartographic future of New Delhi. These maps originate from the Anglophobic work of a Swedish explorer whose standpoint was against the British and India. One need not ignore the fact that the first surveying institution was established in China in 1956, so most Chinese mapping was imported and of dubious foreign origins. The initiation of the rankling conflict of boundary interpretations is based on the map released by Beijing in 1956, which infringes upon 5,000 km of Indian territory. The book by Sun Yat Sen in 1920 was another early allusion to the Chinese standpoint, with the book being titled *The Development of China*.

The Chinese claim through old maps points out that the region surrounding the meeting point of the Galwan and Shyok rivers is the entire Galwan Valley region, and it belongs to them. It is the same place where the Western command of the People's Liberation Army ambushed Indian troops in Galwan. For years, China has claimed the Galwan Valley but if we adhere to the expert M. Taylor Favel, then the old Chinese maps too show the Galwan Valley and the entire western southern region to be out of Chinese territory. Even after the 1962 India-China war, Favel writes that the Galwan Valley region was never shown as part of Chinese territory.

China's 1959 claim line can be traced back to the 1914 Simla Convention, which gave birth to the McMahon Line that separated Tibet from India. Since signing the Simla Convention in 1914, the Chinese never raised any formal objection to the McMahon Line until January 1959, when Zhou Enlai, the first premier and head of government of China, wrote a letter to the then Prime Minister of India, Jawaharlal Nehru. It may also be emphasised that during the border talks in 2012, New Delhi asserted that China must adhere to the border protocols which were signed between India and China from 1993 to 2012. From then onwards, China has displayed varied violations of these border protocols.

Zhou Enlai also raised the issue of Aksai Chin with New Delhi and spoke about the Line of Actual Control with India. Pandit Nehru maintained that the 1914 Simla convention delineating the McMahon Line is the agreed line of demarcation along with the fact that the territory from Nepal to Ladakh has been adhered to along with the customs and traditions of the region from Nepal to Ladakh. On 25 April 1960, an important meeting took place between New Delhi and Beijing, which assumed historical proportions, and no one expected that China would initiate a border conflict on the Indian side of the fence so soon after the meeting. It was declared that both officials should meet often to share and deliberate on the maps, historical records, old releases and other documents about the India-China border dispute. Mao declared in October 1962 that China should overcome the Indian forces through their frontier troops, and the Chinese shall die and be martyred standing and fighting rather than surrender on their knees.

Srinath Raghavan writes in the *Economic and Political Weekly,* "The status of the boundaries at the time of Indian independence is clear from the maps produced by Delhi as late as 1950. The boundary in the western and middle sectors was marked 'undefined'. In the western sector, the British had toyed with various boundary alignments to meet their perceived security requirements. Thus, the Ardagh alignment of 1897 included the Aksai Chin area within the territorial boundaries of India, whilst the McDonald note of 1899 placed it within China. China's refusal to respond to the McDonald offer led the British to make further unilateral alterations as mandated by their changing perceptions." The border dispute points to the inability of the Britishers to initiate meaningful talks on the undefined boundary in the western sector. In the eastern sector, the boundary was shown as conforming to the alignment formalised between the Indian and Tibetan representatives in the Simla Conference of 1914.

When the Indian representative, Radhakrishnan met McMahon, he expressed grief, surprise and disappointment at the Indian standpoint not to challenge and contest Beijing's claims regarding the border dispute. Radhakrishnan and the Indian strategic thinkers of the time maintained that China had already occupied Aksai Chin and would not move from there, so New Delhi compromised on the nation's sovereignty and territorial integrity. Still, the other side of the argument also maintained that "Nehru would never go against the country's public opinion." The McMahon Line, as it came to be called after the then Indian Foreign Secretary, was marked on the map of the draft convention and signed by the Chinese representative. Beijing claims that the Indian and Tibetan diplomats and representatives met separately in an exclusionary manner and decided the boundary between India and Tibet, which continues to be the bone of contention between the two countries.

K.M. Pannicker writes, "The Sino-Indian boundary is usually divided into the western, middle and eastern sectors. The western sector encompasses the area of Ladakh; the middle sector the boundary of Himachal Pradesh and Uttar Pradesh (UP) with Tibet. The eastern sector area is called the North Eastern Frontier Agency (NEFA) – now called Arunachal Pradesh. The boundary dispute has spawned a veritable cottage industry of works examining its historical origins." This template serves as the fundamental premise of the Sino-India border dispute along with a series of claims and counterclaims. These fundamentals have to be viewed and perceived as the ideal template of the differing claims of India and China which can be analysed with cogent analysis.

The Chinese Mindset

It can be maintained academically as an apt assertion that the Chinese are very much troubled and pained by the century of humiliation amounting to Western interference and harassment of their ports and country as a majorly significant factor. The Chinese farmers were asked to grow certain crops as the West humbled Chinese pride and sovereignty. Doesn't it find an echo in the contemporary declarations of Chinese Premier Xi Jinping when he refers to the American intrusion and unofficial recognition of Taiwan/Formosa as a transgression upon the sovereignty and territorial integrity of China? It's an easy argument then that international relations enshrine a repetition of foreign policy decision-making and recurrence of events, peace and war, going by the words of Martin Wight in his seminal essay titled, 'Is there any international relations theory or not?'.

Though mechanisms have been developed and have evolved to deliberate upon the claims and counter-claims of India and China, nothing concrete has emerged out of the post-Galwan Valley incident apart from mutual decisions to demilitarise and de-escalate the conflict. The Galwan Valley incident marked a turning point in the context of India-China ties and the more considerable health of the relationship between the two distrustful neighbours. The *Indian Express* has reported that "The People's Liberation Army had pitched tents and an observation post on India's side of the LAC in Galwan. On the night of June 15, a disagreement over the continued presence of the PLA in that area led to the bloody clash. According to reports at the time, Colonel B. Santosh Babu, commander of 16 BIHAR (the majority of the troops at Galwan), who walked up to ask the Chinese to leave, was maltreated by the PLA troops. This led to an escalation and almost five hours of combat involving about 600 soldiers from both sides." Still, a realisation needs to be reached that merely ignoring the patrol transgressions on Indian territory and their utilisation of propaganda and other symbolic acts need not be comprehended as 'routinized rituals' or commonly observed Chinese behaviour. The Chinese incursions amount to a violation of international law, and, in a similar trend, they have been active in the incarceration of Xinxiang province.

The current status of the India-China border resolution talks was deliberated in a free and frank manner in May 2023 with the Joint Secretary of the East in the Ministry of External Affairs along with Lt. Gen. Rashim Bali negotiating with their Chinese counterparts. *The Times of India* report in May 2023 informs us that "In a statement issued on 24 April 2023, India said that both sides had a free and frank in-depth discourse to resolve the pertinent issues related to the LAC in the western sector to bring back peace and tranquillity in the border areas, which will improve bilateral relations."

The statement read, "In line with the guidance provided by the state leaders and further to the meeting between the two foreign ministers in March 2023, they had an exchange of views openly and candidly". India and China also agreed to maintain close contact, pursue further military and diplomatic dialogue, and reach a mutually agreeable resolution of the remaining issues at the earliest. Government sources said that the inheritance of problems related to the LAC, such as Depsang Plains and Demchok, and will be discussed in later consultations. At the political level, discussions will be mainly on confidence-building measures (CBMs) and avoiding confrontation at the borders shortly." One can argue that ushering in de-escalation and disengagement can lead to better relations between the two nations. Also, enhanced economic cooperation, considering the global strategy of derisking and decoupling, can usher in normalcy between the two countries. Also, efforts can be made through Track II diplomacy, which can usher in people-to-people contacts and involve the entrepreneurs and the academia of both the estranged neighbours. Going back to the cartographic constructs, the maps, as maintained and released by India, are internally recognised and display a stability of intent to negotiate. On the other side of the fence, the Chinese keep on changing their maps and utilise strategies such as shifting dunes as an excuse to change their territorial depictions, which has become a significant bone of contention.

Way Ahead

The India-China confrontation is being approached through the efforts of border negotiations and the differences in interpretations between the 'civilizational nations', according to one school of thought. One approach can be that both countries are involved in talks in trade, economic diplomacy and cultural exchanges while keeping the border conflict on the sidelines. Still, the hawkish school in India asserts that without a solution to the border row, both countries will find it challenging to go in other spheres of alignment too which needs to be understood with more than a pinch of salt.

Both the nations stood firm in the context of the Bali meeting between Prime Minister Narendra Modi and the Indian National Security Advisor, Ajit Doval, who met his Chinese counterpart, and these developments have been hailed as the *Xi-Modi consensus*. How much water these diplomatic parleys can hold in the aftermath of Bali is yet to be seen. The 18th round of border talks was held between the nations in May 2023 at the Chushul Maldo meeting point. The border themes between India and China are reflective of deep-rooted malaise. Both countries can initiate regular meaningful and pinpointed clause-by-clause deliberations so that a sense of urgency and fruitfulness can be inserted into the diplomatic discussions between the defence heads and the diplomats of both sides.

The practice of diplomacy can be the next step. The restoration of peace and tranquillity between the two nations on the border can be a precursor element to initiating substantial dialogue and diplomacy. China has appeared to adhere to gradualism and slowed down the talks, similar to dragging its feet during the negotiations India hosted on 31 May 2023. China has stressed the need for India to place the border theme in its 'proper place' and let the other issues be included at the negotiation table. India calls the Chinese strategy of imparting secondary status to the border talks as 'abnormal', which does not lead to stabilising of the relationship and de-escalation of the strategic environment at the border friction points. New Delhi's efforts to add inseparability to the border question from other issues have been gainfully rejected by the Chinese. Defence Minister Rajnath Singh has contended that there have been flagrant violations of the border agreements by China, which he conveyed to his Chinese counterpart, General Li Shangfu.

The Indian argument is that a rapprochement in the more significant exchanges and relations is contingent upon the solution of the border talks. India might not be comfortably placed without such a meaningful exercise. The Indian argument is that both nations must de-induct the one lakh troops from the border friction points deployed for the last three years, which amounts to a war-like scenario. Beijing has dragged its feet on the de-escalation in Depsang and Demchok, thus slowing down the pace of the corps commander meetings. The Indian Army chief also maintains that the scenario on the friction points on the contested terrain persist to be 'unstable and unpredictable', with a new race to build new and threatening infrastructure on the border. This is taking its toll on the peace-making processes on ground zero.

The Other War' with China on IP Theft

We propose is to unearth the reasons behind China's massive Intellectual Property (IP) theft mostly from American conglomerates operating in that country. Further, we will also discuss why China does it either in the name of collaborating or partnering with foreign firms. The author tries to map out what legal remedies are being adopted both by China and the USA to stop the menace of IP theft. Finally, the research work offers a pragmatic framework to prevent growing cases of missing IPs of American enterprises operating in China.

Before we discuss China's massive IP theft from American and other conglomerates, it is worthwhile to understand the rise of the global governance of IP. It is all but simple to delineate that with the arrival of globalization; we have experienced a borderless world. And in this new realm, we all are fast entering into a newly-defined world of social interconnectedness, economic integration, political mobilization, etc., largely determined by an expanse of information and communication technologies.

Globalization is a multi-dimensional process. From the very beginning, globalization has been regarded as a force and a process which has brought a new age. Globalization has pushed IP and operations related to it to a new high. IP has become an economic tool for global business and development. IP has been rightly defined by the World Intellectual Property Organization (WIPO), the nodal agency of the UN, like this: 'IP refers to creations of the mind such as inventions; literary and artistic and symbols, names, images and designs used in commerce'. More particularly, IP refers to a broad collection of rights relating to such matters as works of authorship, which are protected under copyright law, inventions which are protected under patent law, marks which are protected under trademark law as well as trade secrets, industrial designs and other related rights Further, the Convention establishing the WIPO concluded in Stockholm on 14 July 1967. Article 2 clearly outlines various sections of the IP practiced all over the world. It is well understood that the IP system refers to a set of laws and procedures which is implemented or enforced by established institutions in each country. Beyond their legal concerns, IP rights also aim to promote the social, economic and cultural well-being of a nation. Besides the WIPO, the establishment of the World Trade Organization (WTO) in January 1995 and the very unveiling of the most unique Trade Related Aspects in Intellectual Property Rights (TRIPS) of the organization has completely changed the global IP governance system of the world.

Origins of the Han Tirade

The roots of China's twisting of the global IP system dates back to the onset of its entry into the WTO and even much before, when it started opening its economy cautiously. It must be noted that the West has largely misunderstood the intentions of the Chinese leaders. China knows very well that a new knowledge economy would soon envelop the whole world. And this new economic paradigm would be absolutely ruled by the most advanced tools of information and communication technologies.

Precisely, the 21st century has been already set to overrule or rather replace the other giant economic tools like the hardcore industries of the yesteryears. Alikhan and Mashelkar rightly note, 'Leadership of the world in the 21st century will increasingly be in the hands of those who create and harness knowledge. This century, often called the century of knowledge, is indeed the century of the mind' (2009). Probably, an economically resurgent China might have realised how it could utilise its money, muscle power and manoeuvring ability to the best of its limit to take the centre stage of globality. Though it all started from the early days of the legendary Deng Xiaoping, who was known as the architect of modern China, yet the country's journey to the market economy passed through two other significant regimes of Jiang Zemin (1989-2002) and Hu Jintao (2002-2012). Deng, the second paramount leader, must be credited for his pragmatic approach unlike the founder of the great People's Republic of China (PRC), Mao Zedong, who ruled the country from 1949 to 1976. The quiet and unassuming death of Mao in 1976, and a brief period of instability had helped Deng to take over the leadership of the Chinese nation in 1978 and continued till 1989. Since he launched the opening-up policy in 1978, China has transformed itself from a backward agrarian economy and politically isolated state into the world's second largest economy and an important player with global interests and influence. Since 1978, China's GDP has averaged almost 10 per cent a year and more than 800 million people have been lifted out of poverty. There have also been significant improvements in access to health, education and other services over the same period. Even Jiang's term was equally evincing positive resolves to shape China into a WTO-run world trade order. Both Jiang and his premier, Zhu Rongji, were hopeful that the country's entry into the global trade body would force it to carry out domestic economic reforms in the days to come.[1]

Eventually China accepted far more rigorous terms than any other new member that entered into the WTO. Therefore, the Chinese state media also highlighted that this membership would spur the 'cleaning up of laws, regulations, and policies; facilitate the establishment of an impartial, efficient judicial system. All these steps were suggested to bring much needed external competition to the country's inefficient state-owned enterprises'. It needs to be stressed that China's state-led mercantilist trade regime was proved purely incompatible with the global trade order envisioned by the WTO. It has gradually become clear that the hope of a changing market-led economic order and extensive political reforms in China were largely overblown in the years followed by 2001.[2] Since then, the last two decades that the international community has experienced is a purely robust state capitalist economic model supported by a rigid authoritarian leadership fully immune from any influence from the Western liberal economic. Sadly, China is making desperate moves to export this model to the rest of the world. Alas! there are very few takers.

Finally, after Hu, Xi Jinping, the current president, took over in 2012 and since then, his anti-Western and aggressive economic and military agenda have taken the centre stage of his regime. His great 'China Dream' followed by the gargantuan 'One-Belt-One-Road' (OBOR) has been truly bringing tremors to its neighbours and to the rest of the world. Further, the COVID-19 pandemic and the bundles of allegations making China the creators of the killer virus have made Xi a villain all around the world. However, it is yet to be confirmed by the UN's top health agency, the World Health Organization (WHO), that China is the source of origin of COVID-19. During this pandemic period starting roughly from September 2019 till now, China has largely remained unaffected unlike many of its counterparts and probably enemies such as America, India, Australia, etc. It has surely emboldened Xi to claim that China can overcome great pandemics like COVID-19 and can sustain its growth and development in all sectors.

We can zero in upon three elements which can be mentioned and adroitly delved into in the context of the Han-India relations and related tensions and pinpricks in the partnership. What needs to be mentioned is that around 20 rounds of post-Galwan negotiations have taken place between military officers and diplomats of both the nations; still the intransigent attitude of the Chinese interlocutors leaves the talks at an uncomfortable station with outputs seldom to be seen in the diplomatic outcome. The US Institute for Peace informs us, "Relations between the two Asian giants have soured over the last decade, particularly following a 2020 border brawl between Indian and Chinese troops in the Galwan Valley. While there are credible concerns that these nuclear powers' ties are trending in the wrong direction – particularly as both sides continue provocative actions – neither Beijing nor New Delhi wants to see an escalation toward a more serious conflict. For its part, the USA has sought to deepen its security and economic relationship with India as the US-China rivalry intensifies and considers it a vital partner in Washington's Indo-Pacific strategy. But do not expect India to simply follow the US lead, as New Delhi remains firm on its policy of nonalignment amid rising major power competition and an emerging multipolar world."[3]

The authors further write, " For the present, China seeks to maintain a cordial working relationship with India, setting aside contentious issues such as the unresolved border dispute while it plays a long game to advance its interests. For the foreseeable future, Beijing desires to keep New Delhi contained in a geostrategic South Asian box with the lid on tight. All this while China will conduct business-as-usual diplomacy and commerce with India. Chinese leaders perceive India as an over-sized middle power with great power pretensions."[4]

The authors further contend, "That said, in recent years, Beijing has taken New Delhi more seriously as a threat to national security and an impediment to China taking its rightful place as the dominant Asian power on both the landmass and littoral of a vast continent. Consequently, China has – among other things – doubled down on its long-standing 'all weather relationship' with India's South Asian nemesis, Pakistan. This Beijing-Islamabad continental axis includes sizeable and enduring military and economic dimensions."[5] Thus, one can foresee that apart from the border dispute between the twin nations and the ideological conflict, the Chinese and the Indians are clashing at different scenarios all across the global polity to become the leading Asian power.

In a similar vein, the *Foreign Policy* magazine informs us, "In 2014, Indian Prime Minister Narendra Modi laid out a red carpet for Chinese President Xi Jinping in Modi's home state of Gujarat in the hopes of building a rapport with the Chinese premier and laying a foundation to resolve their countries' vexing border dispute in the Himalayas. But as they walked along the banks of the Sabarmati River and chatted in the veranda of activist Mahatma Gandhi's ashram, Indian media was reporting on a new Chinese incursion in the mountainous region of Ladakh. Hundreds of Chinese troops were staring at their Indian counterparts while insisting on building a road inside Indian-administered territory. The standoff only ended after 16 tense days."[6]

Anchal Vohra further writes that "Modi's numerous attempts to woo Xi – whether through the evocation of hospitality, history, or global statesmanship – have done little to stem China's increasingly assertive claims along its 2,100-mile border with India. This worsening of bilateral relations represents a political problem for Modi, who sold himself to the Indian populace as a strong leader, unforgiving on questions of territorial integrity and national security. Yet he has presided over a loss of men and reportedly also land to the Chinese."[7] This view might be rather lopsided as the Indian Prime Minister has left no stone unturned in the realm of public diplomacy to solve the fracas with China. It can be argued that with the treacherous Chinese intent, the whole question of border talks has taken a beating wherein the two nations are more or less at loggerheads. As is the traditional saying, when a person claps, both the palms must be involved and the Chinese reciprocity leaves much to be desired.

Derek Grossman writes in *Foreign Policy,* "Since assuming office in 2014, Prime Minister Narendra Modi has turned India into a strategic player with a highly effective foreign policy. Modi has done this by shifting New Delhi away from its old strategy of strict nonalignment, paving the way for stronger ties with great and middle-sized powers."[8] It had been a gathering clamour in New Delhi that the policy of non-alignment needs to be replaced with a more contemporary paradigm. Multi alignment is the order of the day for Prime Minister Modi wherein a deft balancing act and disciplined tightrope walk has been attempted by Modi ji. All these steps have been tried in the context of Russia and China relations and the now stalemated Ukraine-Russia war.

Derek Grossman writes in a Rand Corporation report that "Modi has also successfully faced down his country's archrivals, Pakistan and China. In 2020, Modi instructed the Indian Army to stand its ground amid lethal border clashes with China, and India even regained some lost territory. In 2019, after a Pakistan-based terrorist group's attack in the erstwhile state of Jammu and Kashmir, India retaliated in measured fashion – resolve while preventing escalation. Notably, there have been no major terrorist attacks involving Pakistan-based groups since the incident."[9]

Derek Grossman further writes, "Building on these successes, however, may prove difficult for Modi. Pakistan and China have strengthened their cooperation. New challenges are emerging from the security vacuum Washington left behind in Afghanistan. Other fires to put out include a rapidly drifting Indo-Russian relationship and the military coup in neighbouring Myanmar that has drawn that country's regime closer to Beijing."[10] The fact of the all-weather friendship between Beijing and Islamabad, remains as a perennial spoilsport along with the hegemonic and expansionist tendencies of the Han foreign policy. This is attempted in order to normalise the relations between Beijing and New Delhi. With Taliban delegations regularly visiting Beijing for talks with China, the pitch has been further soured for India that is Bharat post the withdrawal of the American forces from Kabul.

It would be wrong to say and contend that Modi ji's foreign policy vis-a-vis China, has not provided Bharat with the much needed lift and dividends as New Delhi has been making all kinds of efforts to normalise relations with Beijing. Still, the unpredictable and scheming nature of Han acts have muddied the pitch for Bharat, Diplomatically. it can be argued whether Narendra Modi brings anything substantively new to Indian foreign policy. This article assesses Modi's record towards Pakistan and China, arguing that he has significantly changed the course of India's diplomacy at two levels – bilateral diplomacy and coalition diplomacy. India has traditionally followed a policy of slow-to-anger, prudential bilateral diplomacy and, in the name of non-alignment, reluctant coalition-building against both the powers. Under Modi, New

Delhi has adopted a more assertive stance bilaterally and has actively sought to recruit third parties into a diplomatic coalition against Pakistan and China. Modi's assertive bilateralism has translated into an insistence that anti-terrorism is the only subject of discussion and that the Kashmir dispute with Pakistan is off the table. In the case of Beijing, assertive bilateralism has meant reversing India's traditional stance of normalization of relations leading to a border settlement by arguing that quicker progress on a settlement must be the condition for any further diplomatic normalization. Modi's coalition diplomacy has entailed an active engagement with the USA, the Gulf countries."[11] The stand that Modi ji has initialised in the context of China relations and attendant politics is the idiom that Bharat has turned and metamorphosed into a harder and more aggressive policy overtures and decisions towards China. This has been termed by Prof. Kanti Bajpai as aggressive bilateralism wherein power throwing and pontificating are the order of the day.

Rahul Roy Chaudhary writes in the journal of the European Council on Foreign Relations "The primacy of the neighbourhood for Modi is clear. Unlike previous leaders, he is eager to use foreign policy as a means to generate inward investment, business, and technology for domestic growth and development. As a pragmatist, he is aware that this will be facilitated by enhancing regional cooperation and stability in South Asia. But it will be a difficult and complex task, especially given India's two powerful nuclear-armed neighbours, Pakistan and China, whose relations with India are marked by tensions and political and military standoffs. Modi's policy towards both countries has undergone significant shifts during his first year in office."[12]

The author further informs us that "For the Indian security establishment, China poses a strategic challenge rather than a threat. India is primarily concerned by China's assertiveness in the border dispute, by its growing trade and defence relationships with India's South

Asian neighbours, and by the expansion of Chinese influence in the Indian Ocean, the latter that India fears as possible encirclement. All this has hardened New Delhi's perspective towards Beijing. But, at the same time, China is India's largest trading partner. Although Modi seeks stronger trade and investment links with China, he has also been tough on his powerful neighbour. In his electoral campaign, he criticised China's 'mindset of expansion'.[13]

Indeed, Tibet's prime minister-in-exile Lobsang Sangay found himself in the official photograph at Modi's swearing-in ceremony. When Chinese forces crossed the Line of Actual Control (LAC) at Chumar during a September 2014 trip to India by President Xi Jinping, Modi's response was robust. He sent reinforcements to the area and ensured that Indian troops held their positions. He publicly expressed concern over the border dispute, and raised the issue of Beijing's policies in the neighbourhood with his guest.

The joint statement issued at the end of Modi's May 2015 visit to China did not reference maritime cooperation or Asia-Pacific security, unlike a similar statement eight months earlier. Nor did it refer to China's One Belt, One Road initiative or to its Maritime Silk Road, both of which India views with suspicion. In June 2015, India declared that the China–Pakistan Economic Corridor (CPEC) project was "not acceptable", as it would use infrastructure in disputed Kashmiri territory."[14] India under PM Modi has seen a perceptible change and transformation in its foreign policy shenanigans with Beijing. New Delhi has become more assertive and smart with the New Delhi denomination not agreeing with the rosy picture of diplomacy being spread around by the treacherous Chinese. There has been reluctance on the part of China since 2014 in a much well-delineated manner to solve the classical border dispute despite repeated entreaties by New Delhi. China has become stubborn and unpredictable as part of a larger obfuscating strategy to stymie the peace overtures by PM Modi.

Eurasia Review reports pithily that "The bilateral relations between the two countries under Modi have taken the slow yet steady route. Modi himself has agreed that while India can 'speak to China eye-to eye,' the objectives of foreign policy lay not in 'changing mindsets' but in 'finding common grounds for converging interests.' This careful deliberation of interests with a hint of realpolitik is also reflected in India's stance over issues of critical importance to China. For instance, while India has been more assertive in demanding a peaceful resolution to the South China Sea (SCS) dispute, in May 2016 it refused to hold joint patrols with the USA in the region. It also explicitly ruled out its participation in any such future patrols."[15] India has largely adopted a peacenik approach to the China problem but akin to Pakistan, the Han have been very taciturn in responses of the diplomatic variant. In a manner, the Indian championing of the South China Sea theme along with the nom de plume of India in QUAD have been resented by Beijing. Indian proximity to Washington too has rankled nerves in the Han diplomatic establishment but apart from all these developments and arguments, India and Japan, Australia and the USA are definitely attempting to contain China in the Asia Pacific. PM Modi has undertaken a laudable and proactive stance to openly espouse the cause of the QUAD with a skilful intent to counter and contain the Han in the near future.

The author furthers states that "This, however, was in stark contrast to India's participation with the USA and Japan in the trilateral naval exercise held in June 2016 in the West Philippine Sea, treading dangerously close to the SCS region. This could be read as a sign of India's assertion of its dominance over the Indian Ocean, while simultaneously respecting China's interests in the SCS. Modi during his recent US visit also gave reassurances that China would not be 'demonized' in view of the developments in the India-USA bilateral ties."[16] The USA needs to play a more pertinent and positive role in the changing and aggressive dynamics of the India-China negotiations. If scholars talk about the Manichaestic portrayal of China by India, then one can divert their attention towards the demonic and war crazy portrayal of Bharat by Chinese reports and their mainstream media, too.

Prime Minister Narendra Modi has espoused an aggressive and tit for tat game with an IR approach in relation to the shenanigans of the

People's Republic of China. Pundit Nehru believed in the swansong of the Han when the entire New Delhi dispensation was geared towards believing in the Han chant of, 'Hindi-Chini Bhai Bhai'. Pundit Nehru's policy of non-alignment with the power blocs of world politics was distrusted by the West and one of the Americans declared India to be the lackey of the communism in the Soviet Union.

The national daily, *Hindustan Times,* reported, "First, a blunt truth. The conventional understanding that the two countries had developed such a close relationship that it qualified the two peoples to be brothers, captured in that evocative slogan, Hindi-Chini bhai bhai, is false. As classified documents reveal, Nehru's friendship with China was one-sided with little reciprocity."[17]

The *Hindustan Times* further reports, "Suspecting India of having a hidden agenda on Tibet, China gave no space, minced no words and told India not once, but several times, that Tibet was its internal affair and it would not tolerate any interference from India. India's lack of understanding of the depth of China's sentiments against the Simla Convention (which determined the status of Tibet in 1914) was a key problem. Beijing argued it had not signed the treaty, treated it as an unequal pact, and blamed it on the imperial legacy. When China squeezed India out of Tibet in the Panchsheel Agreement of 1954, Nehru called the five principles 'wholesome' and erroneously described it as 'a very important event'."[18] Akin to the Chinese rant against Taiwan and the USA and also to the days leading up to the China war, it was misread by Prime Minister Nehru that despite the differences over the territoriality and sovereignty of Tibet, China would desist from any military misadventure against India. This rosy picture scenario turned out to be a Nehruvian dream and worst of all, India was unprepared for the military confrontation.

Indian brave hearts had to pay the price of the Nehruvian foreign policy vis-a-vis China wherein the Chinese nature and intent was misread by the New Delhi dispensation. The *Indian Express* notes in a seminal article, 'These words engraved on the Rezang La War Memorial resonate every time we think of those brave hearts who endured, served and sacrificed to defend India, during the India-China War of 1962. Places like Walong, Rezang La, Tongpen La, Bomdila and Nathula have become etched in our conscience soaked with the blood and sacrifice of the brave hearts."[19] *The Indian Express* further reports, "I have had the stories told to me, of these young men, stoic and determined, underequipped and underprepared being flown into battles at various advanced land groupings (ALGs) by air warriors of the Indian Air Force. They also had to fly the wounded and dead back. They were narrated to me by one such air warrior who flew countless missions to these ALGs and was decorated for it – Flight Lieutenant M.K. Chandrasekhar – my father."[20] Thus, the Indian political leadership was found wanting as Indian soldiers were thrust into the middle of the ongoing fire and brimstone of the battles. Indian soldiers sacrificed their lives and became national icons such as Shaitan Singh at Rezang La. The Krishna Menon-Nehru combination along with B.N. Mullick, misinterpreted the Chinese designs and planning and the Chinese invasion of 1962 turned out to be a military nightmare for Bharat and the nation had to wait till 1965 and 1971 in order to emerge patchily out of the China syndrome akin to the Vietnam syndrome for the USA.

The national daily further reported that, 'China's Marxists seized power in 1949 under the leadership of Mao Tse-Tung. Within the next decade, they annexed Tibet, forcing its religious and political head, the Dalai Lama, to seek asylum in India. The aggressive policy of Mao-led China had already been predicted by India's First Deputy Prime Minister, Sardar Vallabhbhai Patel. In his 1950 letter to PM Jawaharlal Nehru, he referred to China as a potential enemy. Unfortunately, Nehru, possibly influenced by his left-leaning Defence Minister Krishna Menon, was enamoured with the idea of peaceful coexistence with an obviously hostile country."[21]

The *Indian Express* investigated the case of Chinese intransigence and its rising belligerence with India which leaders such as Sardar Vallabhbhai Patel and Golwalkar pointed out to the national voices. These leader's concerns were all ignored which led to the military defeat in 1962. The newspaper reports that "A wide spectrum of political leaders like Ram Manohar Lohia, M.S. Golwalkar, Jayaprakash Narayan expressed concerns about China but they were ignored. The government of the day kept on living in the delusional propaganda of 'Hindi-Chini Bhai-Bhai' while the Chinese further intruded into Indian territory. Post-1953, China aggressively constructed highways, and brazenly and repeatedly violated borders. Their maps, as early as 1954, showed the Aksai Chin region as Chinese territory. To a careful and responsible leadership, this would have sounded alarm bells, but PM Jawaharlal Nehru, wittingly or unwittingly, chose to be misled by his Chinese counterpart Zhou Enlai and went on to sign the Panchsheel Pact. The treaty, presented as the foundational pillar of peaceful coexistence, proved to be a meek capitulation."[22]

Rajiv Roy postulated about China in the *Assam Times*, "Can the NDA government contain the expansionist regime practiced by the People's Republic of China after the blunders committed by former Indian Prime Minister, Jawaharlal Nehru. Whereas, Narendra Modi is pursuing India's foreign policy determinedly from the very first day of his swearing-in ceremony by inviting his neighbours and SAARC countries, he is certainly going to be a stand away from an atheistic Nehru who believed in reason. In his second research, Dr. B.B. Dutta, former Shillong parliamentarian, laid down a complete picture of Nehru's flawed China Policy which earned him and the country an unforgettable humiliation."[23] Beginning from the folly of letting a third party like the United Nations internationalize the Kashmir issue in the Kabailee incursion of 1949 Nehru misinterpreted the olive leaf and the fluttering Chinese pigeon. It was cleverly brandished by Beijing to flummox the Indian strategy makers and the vain political leadership of the times.

Rajiv Roy writes in the *Assam Times*, "He said that when in 1950 China entered Tibet – which Mao Tse Tung described as the 'Palm of Modern China' Nehru failed to read the implications of China's entry. He could not connect through Aksai Chin connecting Tibet with Xing Xiang province of China. This invasion over Tibet was hotly debated in the Indian parliament where Nehru defended himself queerly by saying that in that barren territory "not a blade of grass grows". Mahavir Tyagi, the famous parliamentarian and the great freedom fighter who joined the British Indian Army and then resigned because of the Jallianwala Bagh massacre famously retorted pointing to his own bald head, "nothing grows there. should it be cut off or given away to somebody else?"[24]

As it turned out PM Nehru believed in adherence to what he termed as 'reason' and 'rationality'. The manner in which Nehru belittled the significance of Tibet as a buffer state, had to be borne in a costly manner by the Indian establishment when the Han invaded later on.

Defeats in war are serious business. Countries learn from losses, take citizens into confidence, and move on. "They can also hide behind a wall of fabrication and continue misinforming citizens long after the event. India falls in the latter class of countries. On Tuesday, a key report into the 1962 military debacle with China – which the government has refused to release for more than 50 years –was posted online by journalist Neville Maxwell. He possesses a copy of the report – authored in 1963 by two army officers, Lt. Gen. T.B. Henderson-Brooks and Brigadier P.S. Bhagat. The officers were asked to enquire into the tactical mistakes made in carrying out the war. Their ambit was deliberately narrowed to prevent an inquiry into the shortcomings of the political leadership."[25] The release of the secret papers on the China war has further bedevilled the cause of the Congress regime along with the clarity about the strategic and diplomatic mistakes committed by Prime Minister Nehru. The manner in which the political leadership of the times misread the Chinese side and its malicious inclinations received short shrift from New Delhi which further muddied the waters for Bharat. Apart from this facet of Indian nonchalance and act of an ignoramus, the socialist inclination of PM Nehru too prevented him to sternly see through the Chinese intent and strategic nature.

There was a palpable diplomatic failure to arrive at a solution with China. Sushant Singh further writes that "Until the early 1950s, India was blissfully ignorant of Chinese claims. Maps published in 1954 by Beijing showed the north-eastern edge of Jammu and Kashmir (the Aksai Chin region) as Chinese territory, Instead of raising the issue with China forcefully and taking the country into confidence, the Jawaharlal Nehru government chose to remain quiet. The obvious way out was to sit across the table and resolve the issue. If there was any stage when a diplomatic solution was possible, this was the time. The disputed borders were not delineated, leave alone demarcated."[26]

The strategic folly of engaging in a 'forward policy' of creating military posts in a disputed zone that could not be supplied properly with food, equipment, arms and ammunition, backfired on New Delhi. Beginning in 1957 – India began establishing these posts in areas that China considered its territory, further inflaming what was a dangerous situation. The consequences of this policy were not appreciated. Right up to the point when China attacked Indian positions in the Northeast Frontier Agency (NEFA, as Arunachal Pradesh was called then), Nehru and his defence minister V.K. Krishna Menon believed that China would take no action.[27]

There was a majorly significant strategic mishap in planning as Chinese hegemonic and expansionist designs were not clearly and in a timely manner deciphered by PM Nehru. Historical, classical and civilizational fabrications came through the Chinese standpoint which Nehru negated despite the Han intentions and design. The cartographic aggression of the Han was present in the fulsome glare of the public domain and sphere' yet, appropriate and timely schemata was never drawn by the New Delhi denomination.

In his address to the nation on AIR on 20 November 1962, Nehru said, "Huge Chinese armies have been marching in the northern part of NEFA. We have had reverses at Walong, Se La and today Bomdila, a small town in NEFA, has also fallen. We shall not rest till the invader goes out of India or is pushed out. I want to make that clear to all of you, and, especially our countrymen in Assam, to whom our heart goes out at this moment." Atul Saikia, a resident of Dekargaon in Tezpur, said, "Assam was almost given away to China when Jawaharlal Nehru, in his speech after the capture of Bomdila, announced 'my heart goes out to the people of Assam' on the radio."[28] The façade of the stiff Indian response to Han aggression was exposed by the lax China policy and war gaming of Krishna Menon and the Indian Prime Minister Nehru.

Throughout his career as a diplomat, Krishna Menon had been a controversial figure. He was ridiculed as a Bohemian and a drunkard which was assiduously related to his functioning as India's defence minister. In the initial days of the war, PM Nehru was falsely confident about the capacity of the Indian Army to ward off the Han threat and invasion. As defeat after defeat in the NEFA became the order of the day, PM Nehru stood exposed as a leader who had faith and trust in an enemy which was very overtly giving indications about its aggression and future belligerence.

NOTES

1. Ibid.
2. Ibid. 1.
3. Daneil Markey & Andrew Scobell. 'Three Things to know about China India Tensions,' URL: https://www.usip.org/publications/2023/10/three-things-know-about-china-india-tensions (Online: Web), accessed on 2 October 2023.
4. Ibid.
5. Ibid. 1, Fn. 1.
6. Ibid. Fn. 2
7. Ibid. 3, Fn. 1.
8. Derek Grosmman. 'Modi's Foreign Policy Juggling Act,' *Foreign Policy*, October, 2022.
9. Derek Grossman. 'India China Juggling Act,' URL: https://www.rand.org/pubs/commentary/2022/02/modis-foreign-policy-juggling-act.html (Online: Web), accessed on 1 May 2022.
10. Ibid.
11 Kanti Bajpai, " Narendra Modi's Pakistan and china Policy: Assertive Bilateral Diplomacy, Active Coalition Diplomacy, " International Affairs, Volume 93, Issue 1, January, 2017, Pages 69-91
12 Rahul Rai Choudhary, European Council on Foreign Relations, "Modi's Approach to China and Pakistan," Institute's release, October 2020
13. Ibid.
14. Ibid.
15. Niharika Tagotra. 'Modi's China Policy: Between Rhetoric and Reality,' URL https://www.eurasiareview.com/30112016-modis-china-policy-between-rhetoric-and-reality-analysis/#google_vignette (Online Web), accessed on 10 November 10, 2023.
16. Ibid.
17. Avtar Singh Bhasin. 'How PM Nehru mishandled China,' *Hindustan Times*, 11 July, 2021.
18. Ibid.
19. Rajeev Chandrashekhar. 'India China War,' *Indian Express*, 21 November, 2023.
20. Ibid.
21. Ibid., Fn. 1.

22. Ibid., Fn. 2.
23. Rajiv Rao. 'The Blunderbuss called Nehru,' 11 July 2023.
24. Ibid.
25. Siddarth Singh. '1962 War Debacle,' 19 March 2014.
26. Ibid.
27. Ibid., Fn. 1.
28. Nehru's speech at the fall of Bomdila in Assam, as cited in *The Hindu.*

Chapter Five

India-US Relations: The Notion of Demos Frens...

The Modi Interlude

Ties between India and the United States of America subsist on a substratum of 'shared values' wherein the life practices of the order of rule of law, democratization of tyrant nations and despots, liberalism and avid espousal of constitutionalism amount to elements of foreign policy convergence. On a theoretical level, cooperation between New Delhi and Washington are on a strategic cusp with grandiose adjectives such as 'the all-consequential relationship' along with other sobriquets such as 'a special relationship' as spawned by former president Donald Trump. In this context, Prime Minister Narendra Modi's upcoming US visit is more than merely symbolic in nature and political-diplomatic veneer. The expectations are at a high diplomatic perch this time around as a slew of treaties premised on defence cooperation are on the anvil as an outcome of the PM's trip to the American homeland.

Symbolism and hyperbole are the positive mainstays of PM Modi's diplomacy which is steadily perched upon the instrument of soft power and much uninhibited methodologies in world politics. Then why refute and tarnish them in India? The 'New India' now showcases its power, strength and cooperative inclinations to the global comity of nations and does a successful diplomatic tightrope walk while balancing powers of the order of the USA and Russia in the post-Ukraine war context.

Intelligence-based agreements such as LEMOA, BECA and COMCASA were receptacle elements which formed the foundational elements of an upswing in the bilateral relationship and now a mutually symbiotic partnership. The DTTI initiative launched in 2012 has also been further strengthened by both the nations which will be utilised as an able vehicle to clinch deals in the larger and contemporary context of defence and dual technology transfers to New Delhi for a deeper and much more nuanced strategic and defence partnership between both the democracies of the larger international system.

In his visits to Madison Square Garden in the not-too-distant past, PM Modi amplified and introduced the Indian Dream and the plausible planning which has rendered good consequences for the Indian nation. In his visit to the Shark Tank, Houston, the Indian head of government signed multiple agreements with the American energy trade bigwigs. Later, he hosted the then President Trump at the Motera Stadium in Ahmedabad in February 2020 in order to cement and flower the new realism and moralism imbued partnership between the oldest and the largest democracies of the world. India is embarked on a road to 'Make in India' in tandem with its colossal national objective of Atmanirbhar Bharat which is not a knee-deep and shallow clarion call. The entire striving of the New Delhi denomination is perched atop the 'Make in India' tiger which has begun yielding dividends to the Indian nation in tandem with its larger developmental agenda.

The US Ambassador to India, Eric Garcetti, has welcomed the diplomatic parleys undertaken by both nations which are battling out a transformed and vitriolic international environment. On an official keel, he went on to contend that "We want to help India have the most secure kind of cyber environment that it can because we know there are malicious actors who seek to disrupt, who seek to steal, who seek to weaken the strength that India has. So, first and foremost, we want to build up that capacity. Secondly, for private industry, we've always thought that the right way forward is to safeguard the privacy of consumer data. But we are also impressed by India's ability to take public systems like UPI and others to make sure there is no corruption, make sure that the bottom at the end of the economic scale have access to technology, and through that, access to prosperity."

The GE-414 deal between the two nations is a standout hallmark of the diplomatic parleys between them. The *Financial Express* has noted that the girth of the India-US deal would amount to 25 billion dollars. The present summitry is a follow-up to what transpired between India's national security advisor, Ajit Doval, and his US counterpart, Jack Sullivan. Here in, the transfer of technology (ToT) in relation with the jet engines deal for indigenously manufactured and developed Tejas fighter jets in India, is being reconfigured in the present negotiations between the two nations. The General Electric deal will be an acid test of the mutual trust between the two nations in the near future in a competitive defence industry ecosystem. Given the backdrop of a conflictual Indo-Pacific region, the Indian overarch in the region and its much nearer home maritime space, New Delhi can leverage its air power muscles more effectively. It can be done tellingly through the instrumentality of a domestically produced fighter jet. It will further add to the girth and defence preparedness of the Indian Air Force as an expected fallout of the GE-F414 fighter jet engines. *The Hindu* reported recently that, "India and the U.S. have agreed to initiate negotiations for a 'Security of Supply' (SoS) arrangement and a 'Reciprocal Defence Procurement' (RDP) agreement which will promote long-term supply chain stability as defence sources convey that the deal for assembling the General Electric GE-414 jet in India is 'almost done' with expectations that it could be concluded during the visit of Prime Minister Narendra Modi to the USA later this month." Apart from the defence exchanges, India is also opening up its shipyards for the maintenance, repair and overhaul of American ships; as such, a wider ambit of cooperation and synergy is essentially a requirement of the new challenges brewing up for QUAD and India for the last few years. All in all, the two leaders have in their visions a mercurial imagination of a conjoined start-up ecosystem along with the spawning of resilient supply chains for the future of both the nations.

India and USA are two prominent democracies of the larger

international system. Going by this all pervading and universalising commonality both the nations ought to have acted as a collective bilateral since India's independence in 1947. But the Indian Prime Minister, Jawaharlal Nehru, had a socialist bent of mind which made him formally stay out of the power blocs led by the USA and the Soviet Union. In more than one manner, New Delhi tilted the way of America's Cold War adversary, Moscow. Thus, was initialised a period of mistrust and mutual recriminations despite the political culture of both the nations adhering to the tenets of constitutionalism, rule of law, liberal democracy and an inherent respect and espousal of global human rights.

Public Diplomacy and its Impact in India

Public diplomacy is a spectacle par excellence but never a *tamasha* or mere showmanship for the Fourth Estate. The entire process of foreign policy manoeuvres undertaken by the Modi dispensation falls in the category of sane and controlled razzmatazz in order to serve the national interest. This is an inane comprehension in the diatribes of the opposition. The entire process is part of a larger political interest model which ascertains a riposte from the state actor or the regime of the day. And, as the opposition utilizes the modicum of palsied propaganda and vitriol in order to belittle the global overarch of the New Delhi, new developments unfold dispensation.

The Indian Scenario

Prime Minister Narendra Modi has been treading and initiating a kind of path-breaking idiom in the seventy years of saintly somnolence in the establishment. The tack of an artifice is to market a nation which is already accoutred with the vast and rich heritage and a rich culture which made the outing comfortable for our Prime Minister. It's the art of the impossible which the previous regimes miserably failed to undertake in 'a must approach' of making the *Bharatiya* idiom successfully poised in the larger ideational terrain of global politics. What the New Delhi dispensation has achieved is the larger-than-life artifice of launching forth a surging nation on a pathway of international prominence and resuscitation of its past glory. This is done in order to create a separate and unique selling proposition for Indian morality and age old but timeless ethicality in the realm of foreign policy.

The speeches in Madison Square Garden, the UN General Assembly, San Jose and the US Congress have ushered in the theme of Indian hyper-power in the global arena. International politics is also about staging a show and presenting a badly-imagined nation in a prim and proper manner which the New Delhi dispensation has successfully achieved. The linen shirts of all the heads of states, with President Donald Trump looking engaged as the Indian Prime Minister presented the Indian thought in all its resplendent glory, is a visage that was not witnessed in the past era. The South-East Asian facet is one mere scintillation and the entire aplomb is about tying up with the USA in the larger context. Realism ordains a pragmatic approach and life is difficult for political leaders as they cannot be judgmental in foreign Affairs like an ordinary denizen. This can be achieved through the informal convergence of the QUAD group of nations, namely, the USA, India, Australia and Japan which goes beyond the mere and direct objective of Chinese containment.

The larger professional world which is worth talking about understands the importance of communication which has been brilliantly achieved in a grandiloquent manner by the New Delhi dispensation. It's here in the quaint innovation streak along with global mobilization buttressed by an unparallel presentation which makes the post-2014 foreign policy a successful outing.

The India US Relationship

The manner in which New Delhi has manoeuvred in the context of the Nuclear Supplier Group (NSG) and negotiated New Delhi's entry into the dynamics of the global nuclear trade, is also commendable and has added to the stature of the Indian nation. With the Interim National Security Document released in the aftermath of the first hundred days in office for President Joe Biden, the emphasis is back on re-engagement. It can also be surmised that the importance of values and ethics leading to a larger convergence of democracies and the revitalization of democratic entities too has come to the foreground. President Trump, too, had postulated about the new leadership role of New Delhi which has reached fruition with New Delhi being a dialogue partner of the negotiating parties in the Doha round of diplomacy. Thus, the larger notion of New Delhi finding its way through two hostile neighbours, namely, Pakistan and China requires a new rebalancing by India. President Joe Biden, too, states in the Interim National Security document that China and Russia remain as twin stiff challenges for the USA. Along with India, the USA, too insists on adherence to the ideals of innovation, artificial intelligence and automated robotics, as, a precursor element of American re-engagement. Thus, in the present context of a freshly-elected Joe Biden Administration, cooperation can be furthered in the line of the India's COVID-19 challenge as pressure mounts on the White House to secure India in the devastating pandemic.

With great power comes great responsibility. This age-old adage holds for the American defence and strategic dispensation in a post-Taliban Afghanistan. Americans describe their humanitarian and Democratic zeal in Afghanistan as part of their duty as a super cop and regulator inspired by a sense of philanthropy and service. Undeniably, a part of this valued-based foreign policy outlook is on display in the larger global polity and the regional dynamics of South Asia. One can also cite here what may be called America's responsibility to protect its strategic interests that has served as a quintessential rationale for the long war related to Afghanistan post-9/11.

One can dwell on the Indian context in the larger South Asian scenario. The larger picture of the Indo-US partnership has to be taken into account as it has surmounted myriad challenges from the geopolitical, geo-economic and strategic points of view. There are a large number of instances showcasing the USA's positive intentions in its attitude to India through the decades.

It was US President Franklin Roosevelt (1933-45) who suggested to UK Prime Minister Winston Churchill (1940-45) that India be quickly granted independence. In 1962, then Indian Prime Minister Jawaharlal Nehru sought American help to counter the Chinese aggression in India. President John F. Kennedy (1961-63) was ready to supply India with a squadron of Star fighters and anti-aircraft firepower in the event of a Chinese raid on prominent Indian metropolises. This indicates India's requests were never completely rejected by Washington and Capitol Hill. Also, who can forget the benefits of the Green Revolution when the USA aided India with agricultural and technical knowhow to usher in an era wherein India could become self-sufficient in food production.

Post-Cold War Indo-US Ties

The dark clouds of the Cold War (1946-91) prompted Washington not to cooperate with New Delhi as Indian foreign policy was steeped in the post-independence rhetoric of anti-colonialism, anti-imperialism and rejected the American offer of making New Delhi a full-fledged member of NATO, SEATO and CENTO. Pakistan used the situation to its advantage. Thus, USA soon accepted Pakistan as an ally and Islamabad attained the status of a frontline state during the Afghanistan conflict in the Nineties.

India-US ties had some negative notes till the advent of President George Bush (2000-08) and President Donald Trump (2017-20). The diplomatic and strategic environment changed within a few years as New Delhi signed the Indo-US Civil Nuclear Cooperation deal which gave India the all-significant waivers to become part of the Hyde Act.

On the flip side, one may cite USA negating the supply of uranium to the Tarapur nuclear reactor and trying to browbeat New Delhi on the non-proliferation issue as the latter refused to sign the NPT and CTBT. However, in recent years, the India-US partnership has taken positive turns after the advent of a nationalistic dispensation in New Delhi and former President Donald Trump's ascendancy to the White House.

Indian Diaspora's Rising Stature

Washington and New Delhi have been on the way to become all-weather allies through their strategic partnership from 2005 onwards. The Indian Diaspora's increasing importance in Washington has added more shine to the bilateral relationship. The positive role played by the American community colleges and universities along with the contributions of the Indian Diaspora in the grand American dream are among the key adhesives of the larger bilateral relationship between the two democratic giants. However, the US visa regime for Indian students and immigrants along with the differing interpretations of the Intellectual Property Rights (IPR) remain the proverbial flies in the ointment.

The recent blitz of intelligence and communication treaties has lent further strength and depth to the India-US relationship. Though the question remains whether President Trump was more pro-India or the present President Joe Biden is more persuaded by India's importance in its strategic calculus. The ties between the oldest and the largest liberal democracies, focusing on shared democratic and human rights values have reached a stage from where they can dream of shaping a more prosperous world and a balanced global order.

In the recently concluded India-US Bilateral 2+2 Inter-Sessional meeting on 1 September 2021, in Washington DC, both sides took stock of the progress and developments in the bilateral agenda under the India-US strategic conglomerate. The stew included defence, global public health, economic and commercial cooperation, science and technology, clean energy, maritime security, terrorism, human rights and climate finance and people-to-people (P2P) ties. This has been followed by healthier exchange assessments about recent developments in South Asia, the Indo-Pacific region and the Western Indian Ocean, given their shared vision for peace, stability and prosperity and a free, open and inclusive Indo-Pacific.

The Quaint QUAD, AUKUS Saga

The Biden-Harris Administration has given top priority to strengthening the QUAD, comprising India, Australia and Japan. a priority, as seen through the QUAD leaders' recent rendezvous in Washington. Further for India, the formation of the new Indo-Pacific coalition AUKUS – between Australia, the United Kingdom, and the USA – is a welcome geopolitical and geostrategic signal. It is a strong political resolve on the part of Washington to take on the growing security belligerence from Beijing. It also buys more time for New Delhi to strengthen its maritime security. The policy also seemingly aims at formulating an integrated ASEAN-QUAD coalition in the Indo-Pacific and increasing the USA's potential economic outreach keeping in mind that trillions of dollars of investments are at stake.

Still, the new-found cordiality was absent during the regime of Nehru as the two nations parted ways on ideological grounds making the Islamic Republic of Pakistan as the ideal frontline state of the USA in the South Asian firmament. Francine Frankel, an academic expert on contemporary India, spoke at an Asia Program event on US-India relations during the years of Jawaharlal Nehru's leadership as India's first prime minister and foreign minister (1947-64).[1] The talk examined the broader cultural and historical factors that prevented US and Indian policymakers from achieving a mutually satisfactory partnership. Frankel discussed how Nehru's attitudes and beliefs became the basis of India's foreign policy in a context of polarization between blocs led by the USA and the Soviet Union. Nehru sought to distance India from the power politics of the two blocs, which could lead to war and larger disasters in the nuclear age.

Frankel clarified how Nehru became increasingly concerned at the ambivalence of American support for nationalist struggles in Asia when confronted with competing demands to conciliate European allies still attempting to retain control of their colonies. Nehru warned the USA that its actions caused many Asian countries to conclude that America was trying to become the new imperial power in countries emerging from Western domination. The Truman administration hoped to "overcome Nehru's suspicions that the U.S. was attempting to buttress colonialism and is indifferent to the nationalism sweeping through Asia." Frankel recounted how discussions between Nehru and Dean Acheson, President Truman's secretary of state, foreshadowed persistent disagreements in two key areas. The first was on the need for a quick settlement of Kashmir, reflecting US hopes that an end to this conflict could strengthen a common front against communism.[2]

The second query concerned the recognition of and policy towards the new People's Republic of China (PRC). Frankel asserted that while

Nehru distrusted the motives of Soviet-supported communist parties in the national movements of Southeast Asia. He favoured a quick recognition of the new China and a friendly approach, including China's membership in the Security Council. This was meant to encourage Peking's greater independence from the Soviet Union. Nehru's policy towards China was adopted before the Korean War and it reflected the disparity in power between the two countries as China claimed sovereignty over Tibet. This brought to fore the questioning of treaty rights inherited from the British, including the northern border of the McMahon Line. Acheson, who initially shared Nehru's perspective that policy should get on the 'right side of nationalism', and move towards cooperation with China, was overruled after the onset of the Korean War. The State Department continued to recognize Chiang Kai-shek's Taiwan, and India's policy of advocating China's membership in the U.N. and the return of Formosa (Taiwan) to China, was perceived by the US as appeasement."

Thus, the initial years of Indian freedom from the yolk of British colonial rule, marked a no-return trajectory between Raisina Hill and the White House. It needs to be reiterated that India believed in the rubric of the doctrine of strategic autonomy and Nehru devised it in such a canny manner. The Indian diplomatic divide with Washington kept on increasing with Islamabad getting and procuring all the American goodies including new weaponry, technology and diplomatic leverage from Washington. The Nehruvian foreign policy towards the USA was steeped in distrust of the West. Here in the riding alone policy meant a lot of idealism and a sordid, isolated, no-trust approach towards the biggest and the most important nation-state of the world polity. One had attempted to include India in the powerful alliances of the order of NATO, SEATO and CENTO and it ought to be remembered that Pakistan was always a second choice for the United States of America.

President Donald Trump, during his tenure in the White House, clamoured for the centrality of the Indic standpoint of Bharat on international relations. Along with it, one can reflect upon the idiom that India had a socialistic ideology since the nation's independence struggle which found ample reflection in the nation's post-independence policy. Definitely, if India could have become an ally of the United States of America we might have received all the goodies and the ally hood support of the global super cop. The Islamic Republic of Pakistan played smart and befriended the USA which our prime minister did not during the volatile days of the Cold War.

The Oxford University portal informs us that "Having spent altogether more than nine years imprisoned during the independence struggle and anointed as successor to Mahatma Gandhi, Nehru attained a larger than life stature in Indian politics. The impact he had, has been long-lasting and far reaching. On 6 December 1921, Jawaharlal Nehru was arrested for the first time, along with his father, Motilal Nehru. Jawaharlal was briefly released and then re-arrested. Motilal was released in 1922 while Jawaharlal was released on 31 January 1923. Other periods of jail sentences followed: 19 October 1930 to January 1931; 26 December 1931 to 30 August 1933; 12 February 1934 to September 1935; November 1940 to December 1941; August 1942 to June 1945.[3]

The author further narrates that "However, as will be demonstrated, the existing literature on Nehru tends to be narrative at best and sycophantic at worst. Furthermore, there is surprisingly little that deals with the 1950s in an analytic and systematic way, a period which would seem to be a crucial phase in the transition from colony to post-colonial state. Addressing this gap, the thesis proposes an interpretation based upon a theoretical framework where the individual actor's choices are set within a specific institutional context. Nehru is the 'pivotal actor' given the power he gradually accumulated and thus his preferences, world view and 'vision' need to be explored in depth and detail. He cannot however, be seen in isolation for both during the formative phase prior to independence and as prime minister, contextual constraints need to be taken into account."[4]

One can delve into the narrative which was presented globally by the New Delhi dispensation in the context of Bharat's perspective of international relations. The Indian standpoint was too idealistic and pontificatory in all its contours. One can zero in upon Nehruji's speech at the third session of the United Nations General Assembly: "I feel that today the world is tied up in fears and apprehensions, some of them justified no doubt. But where a person feels fear, bad consequences and evil consequences follow. Fear is not a good companion. It is surprising to see that this sense of fear is pervading great countries – fear, and grave fear of war, and fear of many things. Well, I think that it is admitted, or it will be admitted, that no aggression of any kind can be tolerated, because the very idea of aggression must upset the balance and lead to conflict. Aggression of every type must be resisted. There are other forms of fear; there is the fear of war. In existing circumstances it is difficult for people to say that they will not defend themselves, because if there is fear of aggression one has to defend oneself against aggression."[5]

PM Nehru further related that "We have to defend ourselves, but even in defending ourselves, we must not submit ourselves to this Assembly without clean hands. It is easy to condemn people. Let us not do so. Who are there without blame, who cannot themselves be condemned? In a sense, of us all who are gathered here today in this continent of Europe, are there any who have not been guilty in many ways? We are all guilty men and women. While we are seeking points where error occurs, we should not forget that there is not one of us who is exempt from blame."[6]

India under the suzeirainty of Pundit Jawaharlal Nehru contemplated and objectified an India and a very individually Asiatic nom de plume. New Delhi assumed the leadership of the Global South which was very inane in the understanding that India itself was under developed. It can be assumed that India had only moral baggage to offer to the world sans the material aid aspect of it. After the two nations became close allies, the USA backed New Delhi to take up a larger global role as a leader rather than being a balancer and moralist nation pontificating about the theme of values and ethics in the larger international system. However, the fact is that India never pontificated, but, only adhered to the reactive and idealistic philosophies of its post-independence foreign policy in the 1950s and the 1960s.

When Chinese hordes were invading the NEFA and Uttarakhand

regions, PM Nehru had no other option available but to contact and seek help from President Kennedy as the Indian north-eastern ramparts and frontiers were being rampaged by the Chinese hordes. One of the objectives of Mao Zedong was to humiliate Bharat and Nehru when the empty-casket stature of the Indian prime minister was rising and posing a challenge to the dubious, hypocritical and extreme scheme of things. An Indian national daily strengthens the Nehruvian narrative vis-a-vis China and its military invasion. The newspaper reported that "Former Prime Minister Jawaharlal Nehru had sought American assistance. He wrote to the then U.S. President, John F. Kennedy, to provide India jet fighters to stem the Chinese tide of aggression during the 1962 Sino-India war, according to a new book."[7]

It is always believed as an unwritten part of history that President Dwight Eisenhower and other presidents of the USA spoke against India and were India baiters. Going by that argument, was Nehru correct in rebuffing the American establishment? One archival letter proves the contrary as President Dwight Eisenhower clarified to PM Nehru that America had no intentions to go against Indian interests despite the fact that the USA had agreed to militarily help Pakistan.

> "*Dear Mr. Prime Minister:*
>
> *I send you this personal message because I want you to know about my decision to extend military aid to Pakistan before it is public knowledge and also because I want you to know directly from me that this step does not in any way affect the friendship we feel for India. Quite the contrary. We will continually strive to strengthen the warm and enduring friendship between our two countries.*"[8]

President Eisenhower wrote in an epistle to Nehru that "Our two governments have agreed that our desires for peace are in accord. It has also been understood that if our interpretation of existing circumstances and our belief in how to achieve our goals differ, it is the right and duty of sovereign nations to make their own decisions. Having studied long and carefully the problem of opposing possible aggression in the Middle East, I believe that consultation between Pakistan and Turkey about security problems will serve the interests of Pakistan and Turkey. Improvement in Pakistan's defensive capability will also serve these interests and it is for this reason that our aid will be given. This Government's views on this subject are elaborated in a public statement I will release, a copy of which Ambassador Allen will give you.

"What we are proposing to do, and what Pakistan is agreeing to, is not directed in any way against India. And I am confirming publicly that if our aid to any country, including Pakistan, is misused and directed against another in aggression, I will undertake immediately, in accordance with my constitutional authority. Appropriate action both within and without the UN to thwart such aggression. I believe that the Pakistan-Turkey collaboration agreement which is being discussed is sound evidence of the defensive purposes which both countries have in mind.[9]

"I know that your Government are keenly aware of the need for economic progress as a prime requisite for stability and strength. This Government has extended assistance to India in recognition of this fact I am recommending to Congress a continuation of economic and technical aid for this reason. We also believe it in the interest of the free world that India have a strong military defence capability and I have admired the effective way your Government has administered your military establishment. If your Government should conclude that circumstances require military aid of a type contemplated by our mutual security legislation, please be assured that your request would receive my most sympathetic consideration."[10]

Thus, what the Congress diplomats talked about was the disdain and distrust on the US's bilateral relations with New Delhi. The seed of discord had already been laid despite the 'sympathetic consideration' of President Eisenhower. All in all, the initializing of the relationship at a discordant note laid the foundation of a need for bonhomie between the largest and the oldest democracies of the world system. The American President assured New Delhi and Prime Minister Nehru that the US-Paki alliance will have no dark shadow on the India-US alliance in response to which Pundit ji retorted that "I have never heard of a gun which can be fired in one direction."

In Modi ji's time, the India-US relationship has progressed and prospered in a boundless manner with only the Indo-US nuclear deal being a precedent to the relationship. The relationship is now dubbed as a 'Strategic Partnership' and a 'Defence Alliance' between India and the United States of America. Prime Minister Narendra Modi spoke to the American population and the Indian Diaspora which had travelled far-off distances from across the length and expanse of the United States of America. He spoke about the electricity in the air in New York wherein, the rise of Bharat was elaborated and extolled upon. Excerpts of the speech at the Madison Square Garden is an apt pointer in the same direction. The text goes like this. "The festival of Navratri is meant to worship power. It is a festival of purification. It is an occasion to strengthen our dedication. I have the good fortune of meeting you on such a pious occasion. I am proud that my fellow countrymen who, despite being far away from their land, have created a name for India and have enhanced its glory and honour. Otherwise, there was a time when our country was known as the land of snake charmers. Had it not been for you, had it not been the youth of our country, if you would not have achieved these feats in the field of information technology, then we would still have the same reputation of being the land of snake charmers."[11]

The Indian Prime Minister goes ahead with his same truly amplificatory narrative. "A few years back I had been to Taiwan. That time I was neither prime minister nor chief minister. An interpreter was accompanying me. We had an acquaintance by spending a few days together. One day he asked me, 'If you don't mind I would like to ask you a question.' I said go ahead, I won't mind. But he was still being apprehensive and hesitant. Then he said that I have heard that people in India practice black magic. It is a country of snakes and snake charmers. People still watch them? Is it so? I said no. Our country has undergone a lot of devaluation. Our ancestors would play with snakes whereas we play with the mouse. Our youth are able to shake the world with a click of their mouse."[12]

The speech further elaborates, "You all have earned a lot of respect in America through your conduct, values, traditions and ability. You have played an important role in creating a positive image of India not just in America but globally as well. Recently, elections were held in India. There might be quite a few among you who did not have the opportunity of voting in the elections. But, you were all witness to the results. You surely must not have slept when the results must have been declared. I do not think there is a single individual here who would have got a wink of sleep that night. The Indians in other parts of the world were celebrating much more than those within India. There were many of you who were a part of the election campaign, who had spared time and come to India. I could not even meet and thank them. But today I personally thank all of you for sparing your time and living in the villages for months at end. The Indian democracy witnessed an unprecedented turn of events and you played a crucial role in the final outcome."[13] Then he intoned about the efficacy, ease and the insurmountable record of democracy in the Indian nation which was successfully able to evade the negative prognostication of the Britishers led by Lord Macaulay. Macaulay attributed more than a touch of civilizational doubt about India and seemingly was convinced that the differences, variations and divergences in India would not let it sustain a democratic form of governance and administration after a while.

"After 30 years! You are aware that it has happened after 30 years. India has had a government with complete majority after 30 years. None of the political pundits in India could digest this mandate. The opinions of the opinion makers also failed. Well, the poor, uneducated people of the villages gave the opinion makers a new opinion. These election results have demonstrated the people's faith in democracy and the significance of every individual in democracy. Winning an election is not about assuming power. Winning elections is all about responsibility."

Then the Indian PM reminisced, "I have not taken a vacation of even 15 minutes since I took charge. I assure you that we will not take a single vacation. The responsibility that has been accorded to me in this country, by the people of this country, I assure you that we will never do anything that will make you feel ashamed. The country right is now is in a zealous mood and full of enthusiasm. People of the country want change. The world is progressing towards economic prosperity. Even the poor in India are asking how long they are supposed to be languishing in poverty. Everyone is seeking change. I want to assure you and all my countrymen that the government will leave no stone unturned to change the economic situation of India, to lend potential to its social life and improve the quality of lives of the people."[14] The manner in which Prime Minister Narendra Modi congratulated the Indian Diaspora for their achievements and contribution to the American Dream, was, exemplary and highly venerable on the part of any Indian Prime Minister.

Thus, there is more than a novelty but Plain Jane innovation in how Prime Minister Narendra Modi has envisaged the terrain of India-US relations. J.R.D. Tata referred to the stalled economic growth of India after Independence. Confessing his frustration over the economic stagnation crafted by Nehruvian socialist policies, he had famously quoted, "When I was young I was an angry young man: we were under foreign rule, people were oppressed. Now I'm an angry old man because of all the opportunities that have been missed." This paranoia about India's promised future was shared by other business tycoons and investors of that time as well.[15]

Some thirty-five years later, economic liberalization had happened with India opening up itself to the market. Despite its quizzical spelling, 'Entrepreneurship' was no longer a dirty word for a society deeply wired in socialist programming. And while you switch on your television sets, two middle-aged women, Kalpana and Uma Jha from Darbhanga, Bihar, are seen pitching for investment for their handmade-pickle venture.[16] Indeed, the show 'Shark Tank' India' has caught quite a frenzy among the masses in no time – thanks to the booming start-up culture fuelled by the right policies in the country. But how did India manage to negotiate this change – with high acceptance for a reality investing show aired on prime time?

The portal further mentions that "Aman Gupta, who started his company boAt in 2016, says, 'When we started, India was changing and a revolution was happening. A new India was taking its place'. Setting sail in 2016, boAt is today is shorthand for a durable, ultra-fashionable and pocket-friendly audio products range.' Aman Gupta and his co-founder, Sameer Mehta, have carved out a niche in the Indian market which was earlier dominated by Chinese and German brands. According to Gupta, Shark Tank (USA) has a played major role in realising his dreams and shaping him as an investor.[17] Aman Gupta refers to the American Dream and the Indian establishment is also waking up to the entire narrative of novae strivings and a sentient youthful rising which is taking place in the business and investment ecosystem in the nation, that is, Bharat. We are not aping the United States of America, but, we are clamouring for the Indic rise as the Vishwaguru which aims to improve its own lot and then transcend and accentuate at the global keel with the present context being the Indian ties with the United States of America.

The portal further elaborates about the Shark Tank initiative that "In 2021, Sony Entertainment Television bought the rights of the Emmy-winning ABC series 'Shark Tank' with a view to start its own version 'Shark Tank India'. The show was first aired on television on December 16 and runs on weekdays from 9-10 p.m. on Sony TV. The format of the show is simple – budding start-up firms get to pitch their ideas for funding in front of a panel of angel investors or 'Sharks'."[18] Here, we are not talking about a simplistic and propagandist television serial or a panel discussion but about the notion of New India which respects, venerates and echoes with start-ups and their context of creativity and innovation.

The portal further informs us pithily that "The Sharks who have committed total funding worth Rs. 41.68 crore to 67 qualified budding ventures happen to be the biggest names in the business scene today. The galaxy of investors ranges from Aman Gupta (co-founder boAt), Ashneer Grover (MD and co-founder of the fintech firm BharatPe), Ghazal Alagh (co-founder, Mamaearth), Vineeta Singh (CEO & Co-founder of SUGAR Cosmetics) to Anupam Mittal (founder, Shaadi.com), Namita Thapar (Executive Director of Emcure Pharmaceuticals) and Peyush Bansal (co-founder and CEO of Lenskart)."[19]

A White House release pithily informs us that "President Biden and Prime Minister Modi affirm that technology will play the defining role in deepening our partnership. The leaders hailed the inauguration of the

Initiative on Critical and Emerging Technology (iCET) in January 2023 as a major milestone in US-India relations. They called on our governments, businesses, and academic institutions to realize their shared vision for the strategic technology partnership. The leaders recommitted the USA and India to fostering an open, accessible, and secure technology ecosystem, based on mutual confidence and trust that reinforces our shared values and democratic institutions."[20] This is not a time of technology denial but of technology immersion and the spread and dissemination of technology which can foster a closer relationship between India and the United States of America. This facet has been exemplified by the Narendra Modi regime in the realm of defence, space, critical technologies and technology immersion and space tech cooperation between the largest and the oldest democracies in the larger international system.

President Biden and Prime Minister Modi set a course to reach new frontiers across all sectors of space cooperation. The Indian and American leaders have decided that "The leaders applauded our growing cooperation on Earth and space science, and space technologies. They welcomed the decision of NASA and ISRO to develop a strategic framework for human spaceflight cooperation by the end of 2023. The leaders hailed the announcement by NASA to provide advanced training to Indian astronauts at the Johnson Space Centre in Houston, Texas, with a goal of mounting a joint effort to the International Space Station in 2024. The leaders celebrated the delivery of the NASA-ISRO Synthetic Aperture Radar (NISAR) satellite to ISRO's U.R. Rao Satellite Centre in Bengaluru, India, and looked forward to NISAR's 2024 launch from India."[21] Thus, apart from the space cooperation being envisioned at the level of technology transfer and moving beyond that of the joint development of technology and origins, sharing forms a significant part and parcel of the India-US technological and space cooperation mechanisms. The natural ushering of the notion of Atmanirbharta is the single-minded contribution of Prime Minister Narendra Modi. This key facet is an intelligent manoeuvre away from the realm of strategy, security and the ideological psycho-babble of Nehruvian times.

Welcoming India's Space Policy–2023, "The leaders called for enhanced commercial collaboration between the USA and Indian private sectors in the entire value chain of the space economy. Steps are being taken to address export controls and facilitate technology transfer. President Biden deeply appreciated India's signing of the Artemis Accords, which advance a common vision of space exploration for the benefit of all humankind."[22]

The White House release further informs us that 'President Biden and Prime Minister Modi committed their administrations to promoting policies and adapting regulations that facilitate greater technology sharing, co-development, and co-production opportunities. The leaders welcomed the launch of the interagency-led Strategic Trade Dialogue in June 2023 and directed both sides to undertake regular efforts to address export controls, explore ways of enhancing high technology commerce. Stipulations are present facilitate technology transfer between the two countries.

President Biden and Prime Minister Modi hailed the signing of an MoU on semiconductor supply chain and innovation partnership as a significant step in the coordination of our countries' semiconductor incentive programs. The White House informs us that "This will promote commercial opportunities, research, talent, and skill development. The leaders welcomed an announcement by Micron Technology, Inc., to invest up to $ 825 million to build a new semiconductor assembly and test facility in India with support from the Indian government. The combined investment valued at $ 2.75 billion would create up to 5,000 new direct and 15,000 community job opportunities in the next five years. The leaders also welcomed Lam Research's proposal to train 60,000 Indian engineers through its Semiverse Solution virtual fabrication platform to accelerate India's semiconductor education. Another objective is for workforce development goals, and an announcement by Applied Materials, Inc., to invest $ 400 million to establish a collaborative engineering centre in India."[23]

The realm of materials trade and critical technologies is another related area where initial and dithering steps have been undertaken in a convergent and joint manner between the two democratic nations which more or less are confronted by similar threats and consonant approaches. In fact, it is Prime Minister Narendra Modi in consonance with the American side who has cemented and improved the general downturn in the relations between both the nations which has been the subject matter of this chapter's content.

NOTES

1. Francis Frankel. Woodrow Wilson Centre, 'India and United States: Two Different worlds,' URL https://www.wilsoncenter.org/event/different-worlds-the-united-states-and-india-asia-during-the-nehru-years (Online Web), accessed on 1 May 2023.
2. Ibid.
3. Strategy and Vision in Politics. Jawaharlal Nehru's policy choices and the designing of political institutions. URL https://core.ac.uk/download/pdf/32581315.pdf (Online Web), accessed on 10 May 2023.
4. Ibid.
5. Prime Minister's Speech on the third Session of the UNGA, URL https://pminewyork.gov.in/pdf/uploadpdf/34084lms4.pdf (Online Web), accessed on 28 May 2023.
6. Ibid.
7. Bruce Reidel. 'Nehru's China War,' *The Hindu*, 14 October 2014.
8. 'Speech by President Dwight Eisenhower,' URL https://www.presidency.ucsb.edu/documents/letter-prime-minister-nehru-india-concerning-us-military-aid-pakistan (Online Web), accessed on 10 September 2023.
9. Ibid.
10. Ibid., Fn. 1.
11. Press Information Bureau. 'PM Narendra Modi's Speech at Madison Square Garden', URL https://pib.gov.in/newsite/PrintRelease.aspx?relid=136737 (Online Web), accessed on 10 October 2023.
12. Ibid.
13. Ibid. 1., Fn. 1.
14. Ibid. 2, Fn. 3.
15. 'The Entrepreneurial effort in India and United States,' URL https://www.opindia.com/2022/01/shark-tank-is-exemplifying-new-idea-of-india-start-up-culture-modi-govt/ (Online Web), accessed on 10 December 2023.
16. Ibid.
17. Ibid.
18. Ibid., Fn. 1.
19. Ibid., Fn. 2.
20. White House release, Joint Statement from the United States and India, 21 July 2023.
21. Ibid.
22. Ibid. 1, Fn. 1.
23. Ibid., Fn. 2.

Chapter Six

India-Russia Tete-a-Tete

A lot of political vitriol and umbrage is created when one talks about the New Delhi-Washington allyhood. On the other hand, Russia, since India's independence, has been a true blue friend of India. Russia still remains the largest exporter of weaponry to New Delhi despite the avalanche of weaponry and wartime technology which has been generated by the flow of armaments and related tech knowhow from the USA to India. Ideologically, too, Jawaharlal Nehru had a socialist tilt which is evident by the jamboree on a global scale organized by the Indian National Congress in 1929 known as the 'Congress of Oppressed Nationalities.' Thus, the Indian decision not to be a member of the NATO, SEATO and CENTO made us part ways with USA and side with and tilt towards the Soviet Union of the Cold War times. New Delhi owes it to an anti-colonial, anti-imperialistic tilt of the both the leaders and heads of state in India and the Soviet Union.

India and the Soviet Union were united as brothers of peace and brothers-at-arms since the time India attained its independence in 1947. Though India was never rebuffed by the USA still, the tilt towards and proximity to Moscow became an ingrained reality of India-Soviet ties and exchanges with India deftly utilizing the Moscow-germinated weaponry and other technology imports. An MEA release informs us pithily about the nature and tenor of the ties in its correct and detailed historical context.

The MEA release contends that "Russia has been a longstanding and time-tested partner for India. Development of India-Russia relations has been a key pillar of India's foreign policy. Since the signing of the 'Declaration on the India-Russia Strategic Partnership' in October 2000 (during the visit of Russian President H.E. Mr. Vladimir Putin to India), India-Russia ties have acquired a qualitatively new character with enhanced levels of cooperation in almost all areas of the bilateral relationship including political, security, trade and economy, defence, science and technology, and culture. Under the Strategic Partnership, several institutionalized dialogue mechanisms operate at both political and official levels to ensure regular interaction and follow up on cooperation activities. During the visit of the Russian President to India in December 2010, the Strategic Partnership was elevated to the level of a 'Special and Privileged Strategic Partnership.'[1]

Political Relations

Annual Summit: The annual summit meeting between the Prime Minister of India and the President of the Russian Federation is the highest institutionalized dialogue mechanism in the strategic partnership between India and Russia. So far, 17 annual summit meetings have taken place alternatively in India and Russia. Russian President Vladimir Putin visited Goa on 15-16 October 2016 for the 17th annual summit, which resulted in 19 documents related to cooperation in defence, space, information security, foreign policy, trade and investment, hydrocarbons, shipbuilding, railways, and science and technology. Prime Minister Modi and President Putin also adopted a joint statement 'Partnership for Global Peace and Stability' and a 'Roadmap of Events' to celebrate the 70th anniversary of the establishment of diplomatic relations between India and Russia in 2017.[2]

The Ministry of External Affairs further reports that "Earlier, PM and President Putin held a bilateral meeting on the sidelines of the SCO Summit in Tashkent (Uzbekistan) on 24 June 2016. PM will visit Russia in June 2017 for participation in the St. Petersburg International Economic Forum as the Guest of Honour. The 18th Annual Bilateral Summit will also be held on 1 June 2017 in St. Petersburg.

Intergovernmental Commissions: There is regular high-level interaction between the two countries. Two Inter-Governmental Commissions, one on Trade, Economic, Scientific, Technological and Cultural Cooperation (IRIGC-TEC), co-chaired by the External Affairs Minister (EAM) and the Russian Deputy Prime Minister (DPM),[3] and another on Military Technical Cooperation (IRIGC-MTC) co-chaired by the Russian and Indian defence ministers, meet annually. The Inter Governmental Commission on Military Technical Cooperation (IRIGC-MTC) co-chaired by the two defence ministers and its working groups and sub-groups review defence cooperation between the two countries. Russian Defence Minister visited New Delhi for the 16th session of the IRIGC-MTC on 26 October 2016. DPM Rogozin visited India in September 2016 to co-chair the 22nd session of the IRIGC-TEC with EAM. In 2017, DPM Rogozin visited India for the meeting of co-chairs of IRIGC-TEC on 10 May 10 (EAM is the co-chair from the Indian side). He also called on PM and met NSA during this visit."[4]

Still, despite all the bonhomie and camaraderie between New Delhi and Moscow and the pro-India standpoints on Kashmir and other matters that Moscow has been adhering to, the recent overtures of Moscow with Pakistan and China has been slightly unnerving for New Delhi. A CNBC release informs us that "India's relationship with Russia remains steadfast as both sides seek to deepen their economic ties. But Moscow has also grown close to Beijing since invading Ukraine, and that raises critical national security concerns for New Delhi. Indian External Affairs Minister S. Jaishankar recently said the country was ready to restart free trade negotiations with Russia. "Our partnership today is a subject of attention and comment, not because it has changed, but because it has not," he said, describing the relationship as 'among the steadiest' in the world."[5]

The CNBC news portal further informs that "Russia also wants to 'intensify' free trade discussions with India Despite the display of economic cooperation, India's leaders are 'carefully watching' as Russia becomes more isolated and moves closer to 'China's corner'" said Harsh V. Pant, Vice-President for Studies and Foreign Policy at the Observer

Research Foundation, a New Delhi-based think tank. Russia's 'weak and vulnerable position' and growing reliance on China for economic and strategic reasons, will definitely be worrying for India, he told CNBC."[6] CNBC's key pointers can serve as a key guide in understanding and comprehending the relationship between India and Russia in the presence of Indian adversaries of the Islamic Republic of Pakistan and the People's Republic of China working hard to belittle India's cause, meaning its larger identity and interests in the Asian and global arenas.

The key themes of the order are:

> India's relationship with Russia remains steadfast as both sides seek to deepen their economic engagements. But Moscow has also grown close to Beijing since invading Ukraine, and that raises critical national security concerns for New Delhi, say observers. India's leaders are 'carefully watching' as Russia becomes more isolated and moves closer to 'China's corner,' said Harsh V. Pant.[7] It appears "this relationship is going down from being a very high-value strategic partnership to a transactional one," said Sreeram Chaulia, Dean of Jindal School of International Affairs, adding Moscow's 'tighter embrace of China' does not bode well for India's national security needs.[8] India and Russia have always added a higher valued perch and moral allusions to their bilateral ties. One may delve into the planning and five year governance planned model adopted in India which is largely copied from the Russian model. The Russian insistence on education, growth, development and heavy industry were turned to the tenets of factories and industries being the key precepts of the Indian developmental model and planning, too.

India had taken a tough stance initially in the context of the Russian invasion of Ukraine. China never overtly condemned the Russian war but Prime Minister Narendra Modi did in the context of the great history of India and Moscow. The Carnegie Endowment Centre pithily reports that "The encounter between President Vladimir Putin and Prime Minister Narendra Modi at the September 2022 summit of the Shanghai Cooperation Organization (SCO) in Samarkand, Uzbekistan, captured the change that is occurring in the partnership between Russia and India. Speaking about the Kremlin's invasion of Ukraine, Modi, in what amounted to a public admonition, told Putin that he had spoken to him 'many times before' about the need to rely on diplomacy and take the path toward peace to wind up a war that had caused food and fuel prices to soar. Xi Jinping, who also attended the SCO gathering, did not endorse Putin's war, but neither did he overtly criticize it; Modi did. India, while it has long depended on Russia and still regards it as an important country, increasingly seeks to set the terms of their engagement."[9]

The report further asserts that "The consequences of Russia's war against Ukraine will be felt for decades. In Europe – the epicentre of the conflict between Russia and the West – the war has shattered the remnants of the post-Cold War security landscape, triggered a historic break between Russia and the rest of the continent, and prompted the North Atlantic Treaty Organization (NATO) to fundamentally re-assess its security posture.[10]

This shift follows a long series of milestones in the three decades since the end of the Cold War, during which Russia's relations with the West steadily deteriorated. The key ones leading up to the full invasion of Ukraine were Russia's opposition to the enlargement of NATO to former Soviet satellites, its disagreement with the US overthrow of Saddam Hussein's regime in Iraq, the 2008 Russian-Georgian war, and the annexation of Crimea and the start of the undeclared war in eastern Ukraine in 2014. In other words, an adversarial relationship with the West has been a hallmark of Russian foreign policy under Vladimir Putin's leadership virtually the entire period.

Putin's foreign policy has also been guided by two other objectives: a deepening partnership with China, recently described by him and China's President Xi Jinping as a 'no limits' friendship, and the promotion of a multipolar world in which a coalition of other major powers, with Russia at the helm, would contain the influence of the USA and its Western allies. This concept was first articulated in Russian foreign policy doctrine in the 1990s by then Foreign Minister Yevgeny Primakov. This strategy envisions a concert of major powers that includes India and China."[11]

Bloomberg News further writes that "There is a scenario also that presumes that Russia's dependence on China will grow. However, here China and India will manage their relations so as to avoid further escalation of tensions, enabling Russia to continue its policy towards India since the end of the Cold War. Moscow will do so by relying on familiar tools: sales of more advanced weapons systems, especially on favourable financing terms; long-term energy deals at discounted prices, building on the increase in oil deliveries following Western sanctions and boycotts; and a steadfast refusal to takes sides on the issues that divide China and India."[12] Thus, one can surmise that Chinese proximity to Russia does not augur well for India; it has been conveyed to the Russians. As an instance of the contemporary context of global polity and conflicts, the present-day Ukraine-Russia war made New Delhi do a balancing trick on a tightrope. The Indian EAM went on to scold and castigate the global media and the international community that as India has a historical precedence of transactional quid pro quo with Moscow it cannot completely part ways with it.

Also, as an attendant fact, New Delhi strongly conveyed that India will not impose any sanctions on Moscow in the aftermath of the umpteen American and Western sanctions. India bravely persisted with the import of Russian wheat, barley and corn along with the Russian continuance of imports of energy, oil and natural gas to New Delhi. This strongly standing out foreign policy decision was not meant to antagonize the USA and NATO but it managed to do just that in a limited manner and during a few visits of American officials to India, the American establishment expressed its displeasure at the Indian neutrality despite the defence and strategic partnership between Bharat and the USA. Historically speaking, the Soviet Union was being extolled as a paradise of welfare and good governance. A text called 'Hill of Tulips,' provides a glimpse inside the primary and secondary education in the context of Moscow's welfare model. The text reflects and manifests an idyllic bliss wherein there is a meadowed hill which has a primary school built on its top. Also, as an attendant fact, the entire panoply of the system gets manifested there. As an instance, one can contend that the children, villagers and teachers pool their resources in order to build the roof of the school and finally it is the kids who sit beside the rivulet flowing nearby that they wash their hands and legs and eat their lunch provided by their community. So it is a great example of community life acting in tandem with the entire gamut of the state apparatus.

The Carnegie Endowment for International Peace informs us, "There was a palpable competition between the USA and the Soviet Union in India. With China becoming a communist state in 1949, the USA perceived the threat of communism spreading in Asia and sought to engage India. Participants explained that given India's non-aligned stance in the Cold War, both the USA and the Soviet Union saw India as a market to showcase their respective social and economic models. One can deliberate upon Moscow's foreign policy goals in India using indicators such as cultural and educational exchanges. In the 1960s, the Soviet Union started multiple economic programs with the intention of creating a left-leaning popular front in India. These aimed to influence not only the Communist Party of India but also the Indian National Congress. Participants explained that such efforts fit into a broader Soviet objective of creating a large left movement in post-colonial Asia. The Indian National Congress, which was in power, displayed an interest in cooperating with the Soviet Union to appropriate and satisfy leftist sentiment in India. However, they pointed out that upon the outbreak of the India-China War in 1962, the party expected the Soviet Union to align with China in a combined communist bloc."[13]

The think tank further reports, "Cultural Outreach: Participants discussed how the Soviet Union offered India economic programs in return for a platform to strengthen its cultural presence in the country. They noted that while American public diplomacy in India primarily targeted the English-speaking elite, the Soviet Union adopted a broader approach. It projected a relatable model of modernization that Indians could identify with. Participants underscored that by the end of the 1950s, with the launch of the Sputnik satellite and Moscow propagating Russian as a global language, there was a lot of Indian interest in the Soviet Union's activities."[14] The iconic elements in the Kremlin's power and growth juggernaut happened to be that of communist growth models which found a ready echo in the structure of the Indian National Congress (INC). The communist tilt of the INC was an all-pervasive phenomenon which received a fillip in the days of the Nehruvian era.

The report further states that "In the 1960s, the Soviet Union expanded its educational exchange. Moscow began sending manuals and books for mathematics and science to India to project itself as a propagator of science and technology. Further, several professors, mainly female, were trained and sent to Indian universities. This led to far more Soviet professors working in Indian universities as compared to their American counterparts. Participants also highlighted the role of cinema in the Soviet Union's cultural exchanges in India. There was a shift in the Soviet Union's cultural presence after 1964 – a year that saw the split of the Communist Party of India and the death of Prime Minister Jawaharlal Nehru. Even though the focus of Soviet cultural diplomacy remained on India, given that it was the most developed of the developing countries, the Soviet Union continued to expand its cultural diplomacy across the decolonized world."[15] The series and the spree of the Kremlin's cultural diplomacy accentuated the entire garb of influence in India. As was evident, the INC was greatly influenced by the Soviet experience of foreign policy, diplomacy and governance during the early days of the Cold War.

"M.N. Roy was invited by Lenin to Moscow in 1920 to participate in the second congress of the Communist International. This first appearance left quite an impression on Lenin as he was able to get some of his writings incorporated into the Congress decisions. Roy would become the head of the eastern section on the Presidium of the Communist International and travel to Germany and China to train and then help direct efforts abroad. The delegates of the Second International now included representatives from outside the Soviet Union and Eastern Europe. Roy recalled part of the allure of the event as one in which nearly all the languages of the world were heard in the streets of the Soviet capital. For the first time, brown and yellow men met white men who were not overbearing imperialists but friends and comrades, eager to make amends."[16]

Alan Seiraff argues that "The evils of colonialism were rampant. International party members felt much more included being treated on an equal plane than many in the colonies had felt in dealing with European leaders. Roy attended representing the Mexican delegation, as an Indian party had yet to form. While in attendance, he sparred with Lenin in discussions about the goals and strategies of the Communist International. By citing Lenin's 1916 work 'Imperialism, the Highest Stage of Capitalism,' Roy argued that bringing down the most developed capitalist economies in Europe would be made easier by depriving them of their profit source, that is., their colonies. Roy had impressed the delegates with his intellect and knowledge of Marxist ideology. His truly global vision for communism was well received by the congress."[17] Thus, it can be argued that the communist influence upon the Indian National Congress was all pervasive wherein, the entire gamut of developments and progression pointed towards a kind of borrowed superstructure from Kremlin for the Indian think tanks that were subsisting on an extrapolation from Moscow.

Balwant Bhaneja writes, "The importance of Soviet economic relations with India becomes significant when one realizes that in the 1960s it was with India that the USSR had the largest amount of trade (outside the satellite countries). Before the Fifties, the Soviet Union's trade with India was virtually nil and no agreement of aid was signed. But one notices a rapid rise in figures from 1953 to 1964, the last year for which the figures have been used in this paper. Such a rapid change in economic relations between the two countries within fifteen years is extremely significant. Before proceeding with analysis of the significance of the question, let us examine the causes of the rapid shift of Soviet policy towards India. The causes can be divided into two interrelated groups: (i) Politics and (ii) Economics. Soviet historians trace back their interest in underdeveloped countries to Lenin's time when he proclaimed that 'for only when the Indian, Chinese, Korean, Japanese, Persian, Turkish workers and peasants join hands and march together in the common cause of liberation – only then will decisive victory over exploiters be ensured.'[18] Thus, it can be surmised that it was Lenin's thought to civilize and sensitise the developing nations and the recently independent nations such as India, Japan, Turkey and Korea to imbibe the communist role model of development and progression which amount to an insurmountable concerns for the Indic and the national consensus in the light of the seemingly attractive Communist Internationale. The Communist Internationale was propagated as an ideal panacea for the entire gamut of the Third World nations, with India being no exception to the communist experience.

Balwant Bhaneja informs us that "The active interest of the Soviet Union in India only developed in the Fifties, during the era of the Cold War. Undoubtedly, up to 1961, before the Indo-Chinese war, India was in its heyday, enjoying the status of the leader of the Third World's non-aligned countries. Because of its political stability, non-aligned policy, largeness and strategic geographical position, both the super powers wanted to exert their influence on India. Since World War II, Russia had been competing with the USA to prove that she was no less than her in almost every sphere of economic, diplomatic and military matters. Prior to 1950, during Stalin's regime, Russia had followed a policy of isolation at the governmental level that had deprived her of having any meaningful footing in Asia."[19] Thus, immediately following the fall of Stalin, Moscow embarked upon a nom de plume of influencing the workers and the subaltern class of the developing world with New Delhi serving as an ideal conduit for the communist influence.

Despite the stiff tightrope strategic ropewalk attempted by New Delhi, the initial impression which went the way of the Western community and the international collectivist was that India was supporting the Kremlin's cause celebre of the Ukraine war. *Al Jazeera*, notes that "Since the beginning of Russia's all-out invasion of Ukraine on 24 February. The Indian government, and large segments of the Indian public, have firmly been on Putin's side. Hashtags like #IStandWithPutin and #istandwithrussia trended on Indian social media, and the Indian government demonstrated – perhaps most notably by refusing to support UN resolutions condemning the invasion – that it is not willing to jeopardise its strong ties with Russia over Putin's actions in Ukraine."[20]

Somdeep Sen writes in *Al Jazeera* that "India's approach to the situation in Ukraine is hardly surprising or atypical. Since the establishment of diplomatic ties following India's independence in 1947, relations between Moscow and New Delhi have been shaped by a 'high degree of political and strategic trust;. Across the years, Russia and India routinely took similar stances and supported each other on contentious international issues."[21]

Somdeep Sen further writes that "From the very beginning, Moscow saw its alliance with India as essential for offsetting American and Chinese dominance in Asia. And India always enjoyed the leverage that support from a major power like Russia provided in international politics. In 1961, after India used its military to end Portuguese colonial sovereignty over Goa, Daman and Diu, for example, the USA, the UK, France, and Turkey put forth a resolution condemning India and calling upon its government to withdraw its troops immediately. But the Soviet Union opposed the proposal."[22] Yet another incident of the Russian support for New Delhi when the entire West was reticent about India's police solutions for its errant territories.

The author further narrates that "In 1971, India and the Soviet Union signed the 'Treaty of Peace, Friendship and Co-operation'. The treaty formalised India's alliance with what was then a superpower and arguably ensured its pre-eminence in South Asia. The Soviet Union and later Russia's support for India on the issue of Kashmir has also been unrelenting and politically significant. In 1955, declaring support for Indian sovereignty over Kashmir, Soviet leader Nikita Khrushchev said, 'We are so near that if ever you call us from the mountain tops we will appear at your side.' Since then, Moscow has been a bulwark against international intervention in Kashmir. The Soviet Union vetoed UN Security Council resolutions in 1957, 1962 and 1971 that called for international intervention in Kashmir, insisting that it is a bilateral issue that needs to be solved through negotiations between India and Pakistan. And it took a similar stance on the Indo-Pak conflict in general. Such a stance was appreciated across the political spectrum in India."[23] We might be joining the American bandwagon in the contemporary context but still the argument for a soft corner for Russia, despite its Ukrainian invasion, remains as a core stress and emphasis of the India-Russia strategic partnership which was achieved during the reign of Prime Minister Atal Bihari Vajpayee.

The write-up further informs that "In 1978, the then Foreign Minister Atal Bihari Vajpayee – a founding member of the right-wing Hindu nationalist Bharatiya Janata Party (BJP) who served as India's prime minister between 1998 and 2004 – for example, put aside his ideological differences with the Soviet Union, and greeted a Soviet delegation to India saying, 'our country found the only reliable friend in the Soviet Union alone'. Since the fall of the Soviet Union, Russia has worked to maintain its special relationship with India. In 2000, Russia's President Vladimir Putin and then Prime Minister Vajpayee signed a 'Declaration of Strategic Partnership'. In 2010, marking a decade of this strategic partnership, both countries signed the 'Special and Strategic Partnership'. As part of this special partnership, Russia reaffirmed its pro-India stance on Kashmir. In 2019, when India scrapped Article 370 of its Constitution that gave Jammu and Kashmir special status, the Modi government faced severe criticism in the international arena, but Russia once again deemed this to be an 'internal matter' for India."[24] Thus, apart from Moscow, very few nations in the larger international system supported New Delhi as far as the abrogation of Article 370 in the state of Jammu and Kashmir is concerned. Most of the Western nations and the larger community of the global polity did not see through the Chinese and Pakistan's designs on India but Kremlin firmly adhered to a line of support to New Delhi.

The Indian daily, *The Hindu,* reports crucially and tersely that "Prime Minister Narendra Modi has been praised by Vladimir Putin and he expressed the view that New Delhi was firmly behind reforms and palliative and ameliorative solutions for a nation which was blocking its own rise and development, a few years back. Russian President Vladimir Putin has lavished praise on Prime Minister Narendra Modi for his tough stance on defending India's national interests without being 'intimidated' by any pressure and said the policy pursued by him is the 'main guarantor' of the progressively developing bilateral ties. Mr. Putin's comments came at the 'Russia Calling!' forum."[25]

The Russian leader said he "cannot imagine that Modi could be frightened, intimidated or forced to take any actions, steps, decisions that would be at variance with the national interests of India and the Indian people". He said relations between Russia and India are developing in all areas. Mr. Putin, who on Friday announced his intention to run for the presidency again in 2024, said he can feel pressure on Mr. Modi from unfriendly countries. He disclosed that he and Mr. Modi never even discussed this subject, the Russian News Agency *TASS* reported. "I just look at what is happening from the outside, and sometimes, frankly speaking, I am even surprised at his tough stance on defending the national interests of the Indian state," the Russian president stressed. India has been criticised by the Western countries for charting its own course in the face of Western sanctions against Russia for its invasion of Ukraine and continuing its import of discounted Russian crude oil."[26] Thus, as China gives the nomenclature to Pakistan as an 'all-weather friend,' Kremlin views India as an ally which it has always supported and propped up wherever possible. It is because of the Russian slant towards New Delhi that most of the political, civil societal and diplomatic vitriol has been ably diverted towards ire and leading to Cold War disillusionment and disgruntlement with the USA.

Swaran Singh writes in *First Post* that "Where do such polemics put the world's largest democracy, India, and also its 'proactive neutrality' foreign policy posture in the Ukraine war? Western studies continue to club this largest democracy in the world with China, Iran and Turkey which have so far refused to condemn the Russian invasion of their neighbouring nation. Is that a fair comparison and does such labelling of India make Russia any more at ease with India's neutral posture?"[27] Thus, the new term which has been invented is that of proactive neutrality wherein the Indian standpoint in the context of the Russian invasion of Ukraine has been amply appreciated in the comity of states and other international organizations and international institutions. India has desisted from criticizing and castigating Moscow for its military and special operations as Vladimir Putin calls it and thus earned remarkable respect and veneration for its multi-alignment.

Swaran Singh further states, "How has the rest of the world

responded to India asserting its national interest and refusing to toe any line whether Russian or American? Even India's critics agree that its visibility in global politics has increased by leaps and bounds. But in spite of its regular connection with the national leaders of both Russia and Ukraine and its humanitarian assistance for the latter, has India not been able to play any substantive role in resolving this war? Now, this has also come to be not just an expectation but a prerequisite if India has to ensure all 19 national leaders attend India's G20 summit scheduled for coming September."[28]

National Public Radio raised the voice about India's proactive neutrality as India did not criticize or censure its old ally, Moscow, in the aftermath of its invasion of Ukraine and the massive collateral damage which ensued in beleaguered Ukraine. It spilled the beans on India's stance on the Russian invasion of Kyiv which nearly turned into rubble in the light of the massive bombardment and missile attack by Moscow in an anticipation of a quick victory over the desires and strength of Zelensky. But, it was not to be as the entire NATO group and the America-led European comity of nations ganged up against Moscow with an unparalleled and remarkably effective show of strength and solidarity. NPR reports that "India was still under British colonial rule when Russia opened its first consulate there in 1900 in Mumbai. But relations really took off during the Cold War. It started out as strategic sympathy for the Soviet Union, against the backdrop of India getting independence from the British. So it's an anti-colonial experience, anti-imperialism," says Rajeswari (Raji) Pillai Rajagopalan, a political scientist at the Observer Research Foundation in New Delhi. "And as the Cold War picked up, it became a more anti-West, anti-U.S. sentiment they shared." The end of the Cold War did not change that. Neither has the Ukraine war. India's nationalist TV news channels often accuse the USA – rather than Russia – of doing more to ruin Ukraine."[29]

India has one of the fastest-growing economies in the world. (The IMF forecasts 6.8 per cent growth for India this year, compared to just 1.6 per cent for the USA). By 2030, India is forecast to be the third-largest economy in the world, behind the USA and China.

It is already the third-largest oil consumer in the world. And it needs even more to fuel all that growth. But because India has few oil and gas reserves of its own, most of the oil it needs has to be imported. It is also a relatively poor country, particularly sensitive to price. That's where Russia comes in. India still buys more oil from Middle Eastern countries than Russia. But its Russian share has skyrocketed. In December, India imported 1.2 million barrels of Russian crude. That's a whopping 33 times more than a year earlier. In January, the share of Russian crude rose to 28 per cent of India's oil imports – up from just 0.2 per cent before Moscow's invasion of Ukraine.

National Public Radio further reports that "Indian officials have defended those purchases by saying it's their job to find bargains for their citizens. And Jaishankar, the Foreign Minister, has suggested it's hypocritical of wealthier Westerners to ask them not to. Europe has managed to reduce its imports [of Russian gas] while doing it in a manner that is comfortable, Jaishankar told an Austrian TV channel last month. 60,000 Euros or whatever is your per capita income, you're so caring about your population. I have a population at 2,000 dollars [per capita annual income]. I also need energy, and I am not in a position to pay high prices for oil."[30] In a manner, the India-Russia relations stand on the firmest and most sturdy footing as far as India's tete-a-tete with any of its partners is concerned.

India and Russia have been all-weather friends and since the formalised alliance of the 1971 Treaty of Friendship, both the nations have served together as intertwining branches of a creeper due to shared interests. Whether it is the India-China war and its dark shadow on New Delhi's establishment along with the India-Pakistan wars of 1965 and 1971, Russia has always stood by New Delhi but the gung ho and bravado of Vladimir Putin in Ukraine has muddied the turf for India. As New Delhi has not condemned the Russian invasion of Ukraine, the White House too has expressed its displeasure towards the Indian foreign policy decision of keeping on buying much-needed oil from the Kremlin along with remaining neutral in the war. It can be surmised pretty conveniently that India has not bowed down to American pressure of diplomatically assailing a belligerent and bellicose Moscow despite India being a co-parishioner with the White House.

NOTES

1. MEA release, 'India Russia Relations',URL https://www.mea.gov.in/Portal/ForeignRelation/India_Russia_May.pdf (Online Web), accessed on 10 December 2023.
2. Ibid.
3. Ibid., Fn. 1.
4. Ibid., Fn. 2.
5. Sumathi Bala. 'India's Ties with Russia Remain Steady,' URL https://www.cnbc.com/2023/05/03/india-russia-ties-under-scrutiny-as-moscow-moves-closer-to-china.html (Online Web), accessed on 10 October 2023.
6. Ibid.
7. Ibid., Fn. 1.
8. Ibid., Fn. 2.
9. Rajan Menon & Eugene Rumer. 'Russia and India: A New Chapter,' URL https://carnegieendowment.org/2022/09/20/russia-and-india-new-chapter-pub-87958 (Online Web), accessed on 10 November, 2023.
10. North Atlantic Treaty Organization. 'NATO 2022 Strategic Concept,' (NATO), 29 June 2022, https://www.nato.int/nato_static_fl2014/assets/pdf/2022/6/pdf/290622-strategic-concept.pdf
11. *Bloomberg News*. 'China Envoy Says Xi-Putin Friendship Actually Does Have a Limit,' Bloomberg, 24 March 2022, https://www.bloomberg.com/news/articles/2022-03-24/china-envoy-says-xi-putin-friendship-actually-does-have-a-limit#
12. Ibid.
13. Carnegie Endowment for International Peace. 'The Soviet Union's Public Diplomacy during the early Cold War Years,' https://carnegieendowment.org/2023/05/04/soviet-union-s-public-diplomacy-in-india-during-early-cold-war-event-8143 (Online Web), accessed on 10 May 2023.
14. Ibid.
15. Ibid., Fn. 1.
16. Alan Sielaff. *Soviet Influence in British India: Intelligence and Paranoia within Imperial Government in the Interwar Years,* University of Colorado, Department of History, Spring, 2011.
17. Ibid.
18. Balwant Bhaneja. 'Soviet Foreign Aid to India,' https://www.asj.upd.edu.ph/mediabox/archive/ASJ-08-03-1970/bhaneja-soviet-foreign-aid-india.pdf (Online Web), accessed on 10 December 10, 2023.
19. Ibid.
20. Somdeep Sen. 'Why is India Standing with Russia,' URL https://www.aljazeera.com/opinions/2022/3/14/why-is-istandwithputin-trending-in (Online Web), accessed on 10 December 2023.
21. Ibid.
22. Ibid., Fn. 1.
23. Ibid., Fn. 2.

24. Ibid., Fn. 3.
25. *The Hindu*, 9 December, 2023.
26. Ibid.
27. Swaran Singh. 'Why Ukraine War is an inflection Point for India's Foreign Policy,' URL https://www.firstpost.com/opinion/why-ukraine-war-is-an-inflection-point-for-indias-foreign-policy-12194892.html (Online Web), accessed on 10 May 2023.
28. Ibid.
29. Lauren Frayer. 'A Year Into Ukraine War, the oldest Democracy in the World won't say a Word,' Transcript of NPR in February 2023.
30. Ibid.

Chapter Seven

Nehru and the Crests and Troughs Tide of the Disarmament Narrative

The larger comity of states and the international community both at the levels of the hoi polloi, the domestic regime of the day and the labyrinth of international organizations and institutions have laboured under the motif and the acerbic reality of war and conflict. Along with the threat of war, humankind has been striving for a weapon-free world wherein the Hague Conventions of 1899 and 1907, leading up to the fourteen points of Woodrow Wilson and the creation of the United Nations as an antithetical force against the ravages of unbridled war through both conventional and non-conventional weapons, has been the key factor in international politics.

Indian Prime Minister Nehru laboured under the mirage that India was the leader of the Third World which was taken to the extreme of ivory tower zealotry. India became the peacenik nation along with ably supporting and propagating President Dwight Eisenhower's masterstroke in the form of the Atoms for Peace Programme in the 1950s. The fundamentals of the Atom's for Peace Plan was adhered to by India in letter and spirit before faltering at the military confrontation with PRC in 1962.

President Dwight D. Eisenhower was determined to solve the 'the fearful atomic dilemma' by finding some way by which 'the miraculous inventiveness of man' would not be dedicated to his death, but consecrated to his life in his Atoms for Peace speech before the United Nations General Assembly on 8 December 1953. The Eisenhower archives inform us that "President Eisenhower sought to solve this terrible problem by suggesting a means to transform the atom from a scourge into a benefit for mankind. Although not as well known as his warning about the 'military industrial complex,' voiced later in his farewell radio and television address to the American people, President Eisenhower's Atoms for Peace speech embodied his most important nuclear initiative as President. From it sprang a panoply of peaceful atomic programs.[1]

The Atom's for Peace Programme further stressed that "With it, President Eisenhower placed the debate over the control of nuclear science and technology, which had largely been the province of government officials and contractors, squarely before the public. Indeed, the present public controversy over nuclear technology and its role in American society can be traced back to President Eisenhower's determination that control of nuclear science was an issue for all Americans. The Atoms for Peace speech reflected the President's deep concern about 'Atoms for War.' The escalating nuclear arms race between the USA and the Soviet Union, which included the development of thermonuclear bombs, brought President Eisenhower to the United Nations. Since Hiroshima, the destructive power of nuclear weapons had increased dramatically. Nuclear weapons technology, thus far a product of American expertise, would also eventually enter the arsenals of the Soviet Union through the normal processes of technological development. President Eisenhower felt a moral imperative to warn the American people and the world of this new reality."[2]

Rapid strides in nuclear weapons in nuclear weapons technology had begun at the end of World War II. In 1945, the two atomic bombs dropped on Japan had killed an estimated 106,000 people and had injured approximately 110,000 others. The larger of the two, the Nagasaki bomb, had released the explosive equivalent of 23,000 tons of TNT.[3] In 1948, the USA had tested even larger atomic bombs in the Pacific, and by 1949 the Soviet Union had achieved its own nuclear capability with the detonation of a nuclear device. In response to the Soviet atomic bomb program, the USA had embarked upon a crash program to develop an even larger weapon, the hydrogen bomb, which promised explosive power in the range of millions of tons of TNT. The USA successfully detonated a hydrogen device in November 1952, just a few days before Eisenhower won the presidency. The awesome 10-megaton blast had destroyed the test island of Elugelab, creating an underwater crater 1,500 yards in diameter. With it the USA and the world entered the thermonuclear age.[4]

India under Nehru prided itself in championing the cause of de-weaponsisation, disarmament and non-proliferation of weapons. PM Nehru had gone on to contend that "Some of us have talked about non-violence. Do we all believe fully in non-violence, taking it to its utmost conclusions? I suppose not. We are not all pacifists. The word 'Gandhian' is being used more and more frequently nowadays, and by frequent use it has lost all meaning, so that the most violent of men call themselves Gandhian. We all of us had the privilege of serving Gandhi, but I think it would be a little presumptuous on my part, for instance, to call myself a Gandhian. I am powerfully influenced by what he said, by what he taught us. But he was too big a man – let us recognise it. We live in his glory, in the glory of his name. We, in India, take the name of the Buddha and Gandhi and think we have done our duty."[5] Thus, the morality narrative along with the nation's higher perch of values was propagated by India under the suzerainty of Prime Minister Nehru in the context of the non-proliferation of weapons and disarmament of the larger comity of nations and their military units. Often India alluded to itself being the land of Gandhi and Lord Buddha and thus sought the mantle of the developing and the underdeveloped states of the global polity. But, did New Delhi have the girth, strength and potential to stymie the tide of the weaponisers? Most of the strategic thinkers of the time missed this million-dollar question.

Prime Minister Nehru further stated that "We assume vicariously, to some, extent, the virtues of the Buddha and Gandhi, just as to some extent in the West, fierce and brutal wars were fought in the name of

Christ. The tremendous problem which faces the world today is one of survival; one of not being gradually reduced to the level of beasts; one of the increase of civilization, of moral values. It does not require any argument for all of us to know that a nuclear war not only means the end. The destruction of humanity, but that it is something infinitely degrading to our sense of values. Nobody surely can like being liquidated or having any part in this widespread destruction. But, nevertheless, large numbers of people are prepared to put up with this eventuality because presumably they think that something worse may take place unless they are ready for a nuclear war. They are afraid of defeat by another country, and, therefore, resign themselves to an arms race and the possibility of a nuclear war."[6] Nehru recognized that acquiring armaments and the WMDs (Weapons of Mass Destruction) were the order of the day thus engulfing the nations into an irreversible and madcap race of weapons aggrandizement. The world would have awaited a dystopia if the nuclear weapons were triggered in a post-COVID and Artificial Intelligence world of contemporary times.

Or else, they satisfy themselves by saying that nobody wants a nuclear war, but that they must have nuclear bombs as deterrents to prevent the other party from using them. This is curious logic – and meanwhile we go nearer to the final explosion. It is all these bombs that are being made and collected, and all these tests that are gradually bringing the probability of an explosion nearer. And time is limited, if you don't put an end to it soon enough, it may later on be beyond the capacity of human beings or nations to stop the rot."[7]

PM Nehru further elaborated upon his non-proliferation with both the haves and the have nots of the nuclear comity. He said that "The global interest is in having areas, atom-free areas, in Asia, in Africa, in Europe, which are recognised to have no nuclear weapons and which will not be used for nuclear warfare. All this cannot mean much, because the ultimate thing is having no war, full disarmament. But all these are steps which help. Today, the worst thing is the terrible tension and the fear behind it. Imagine thousands of aircraft with nuclear bombs always being in the air day and night. Imagine also those thousands of aircraft being piloted by brave young men. Any one of them may lose his nerve and do something which may lead to a war. It is horrible thought and still on goes this mad race."[8] He too cited the notion of unbridled fear and threat to peace which have been shared in the objectives of the hallowed portals of United Nations Organization. He mentioned the stealth and the expansive strength of the delivery vehicles of the nukes and raised a very pertinent poser what would have happened if one of the fliers of the nuke-carrying weapons wavered in his mental maturity; then a massive tragedy awaited the region and the larger mankind too.

Let's delve into the Preamble of the United Nations Organization which can serve as an ideal platform of moral vows from which the Modian and Nehruvian approach to non-proliferation and disarmament can be conveniently gleaned. The objectives are as follows:

Article 1

The purposes of the United Nations are:

1. To maintain international peace and security, and to that end, to take effective collective measures for the prevention and removal of threats to peace, and for the suppression of acts of aggression or other breaches of peace, and to bring about by peaceful means, and in conformity with the principles of justice and international law, adjustment or settlement of international disputes or situations which might lead to a breach of the peace;[9]
2. To develop friendly relations among nations based on respect for the principle of equal rights and self-determination of peoples, and to take other appropriate measures to strengthen universal peace;
3. To achieve international co-operation in solving international problems of an economic, social, cultural, or humanitarian character, and in promoting and encouraging respect for human rights and for fundamental freedoms for all without distinction as to race, sex, language, or religion; and[10]
4. To be a centre for harmonizing the actions of nations in the

attainment of these common ends.[11]

Article 2

The Organization and its Members, in pursuit of the Purposes stated in Article 1, shall act in accordance with the following Principles.

1. The Organization is based on the principle of the sovereign equality of all its Members.
2. All Members, in order to ensure to all of them the rights and benefits resulting from membership, shall fulfil in good faith the obligations assumed by them in accordance with the present Charter.[12]
3. All Members shall settle their international disputes by peaceful means in such a manner that international peace and security, and justice, are not endangered.
4. All Members shall refrain in their international relations from the threat or use of force against the territorial integrity or political independence of any state, or in any other manner inconsistent with the Purposes of the United Nations.
5. All Members shall give the United Nations every assistance in any action it takes in accordance with the present Charter, and shall refrain from giving assistance to any state against which the United Nations is taking preventive or enforcement action.
6. The Organization shall ensure that states which are not Members of the United Nations act in accordance with these Principles so far as may be necessary for the maintenance of international peace and security.[13] (Thus, the scourge and the menace of war had to be settled and the abolition of war happened to be the keynote element of the strategy of the warring and on the tenterhook nations).
7. Nothing contained in the present Charter shall authorize the United Nations to intervene in matters which are essentially within the domestic jurisdiction of any state or shall require the Members to submit such matters to settlement under the present

> Charter; but this principle shall not prejudice the application of enforcement measures.[14] (Thus, it can be noted here that non-intervention by powerful nations inside the going-ons of the developing and Third World states happened to be the panacea that the United Nations offered to the rest of the tense, and war-tethered world.)

Prime Minister Modi on the other hand, decades later, objectified the time tested discourse of non-proliferation and disarmament and despite the Western and Chinese opposition, India could become a member of the NSG (Nuclear Supply Group). Since the advent of an independent India, India gradually attempted to move away from the agrarian model of growth and development. Industrialization replaced the agri-mould. Still, the fallouts of modernity and the fast-paced mode of development led to the spawning of the novae challenges both in the domestic and security spheres. One of them was the nuanced debate surrounding nuclear non-proliferation and disarmament. Since the heady days of the deep freeze of the Cold War, the international system has been divided into the separating line of nuclear powers and nuclear have nots.

The great powers of the order of the USA, the United Kingdom, France, China and Russia emerged as the grandiose arbiters of threshold states such as India and Israel. The Indian intransigence was very much marked by its resistance to be part of the rubric of treaties such as CTBT and NPT. Though India is only a de facto member of the CTBT, still it remains wedded to the idiom of non-testing of nuclear weapons. India managed a feat of diplomacy vis-a-vis its entry into the Nuclear Suppliers grouping is concerned. The Nuclear Suppliers Group (NSG) is a group of nuclear supplier countries that seeks to contribute to the non-proliferation of nuclear weapons through the implementation of two sets of guidelines for nuclear exports and nuclear-related exports.[15]

The NSG guidelines also contain the so-called 'Non-Proliferation Principle,' adopted in 1994, whereby a supplier, notwithstanding other provisions in the NSG guidelines, authorises a transfer only when satisfied that the transfer would not contribute to the proliferation of nuclear weapons. The Non-Proliferation Principle seeks to cover the rare but important cases where adherence to the NPT or to a Nuclear Weapon Free Zone Treaty may not by itself be a guarantee that a State will consistently share the objectives of the Treaty or that it will remain in compliance with its Treaty obligations.[16]

The NSG guidelines are consistent with, and complement, the various international, legally binding instruments in the field of nuclear non-proliferation. These include the Treaty on the Non-Proliferation of Nuclear Weapons (NPT), the Treaty for the Prohibition of Nuclear Weapons in Latin America (Treaty of Tlatelolco), the South Pacific Nuclear-Free-Zone Treaty (Treaty of Rarotonga), the African Nuclear-Weapon-Free Zone Treaty (Treaty of Pelindaba), the Treaty on the Southeast Asia Nuclear-Weapon-Free Zone (Treaty of Bangkok), and the Central Asian Nuclear-Weapon-Free Zone Treaty (Treaty of Semipalatinsk).[17]

India under the chaperoning of Prime Minister Narendra Modi and EAM, Mrs. Sushma Swaraj attained the better of the exchanges in NSG membership despite consistent vetoing by national establishments of Pakistan and the PRC. The Biden Administration has reaffirmed its support for India's membership in the 48-member Nuclear Suppliers Group (NSG) and reiterated its commitment "to continue engagement with like-minded partners to advance this goal", according to the Modi-Biden agreement document released by the White House on 22 June.

As of today, India is not a member of the NSG, the main reason being its refusal to sign the Nuclear Non-Proliferation Treaty (NPT).[18]

Far more than all other states that have joined the NSG during the last four decades, India's rationales and motives for seeking membership have given rise to questions and even suspicions. This is for two reasons: Unlike all NSG participants, India is not a party to the Treaty on the Non-Proliferation of Nuclear Weapons (NPT); for the greater part of the NSG's history, India deplored proliferation trade controls as a neo-colonialist, even racist tool of humiliation and discrimination used by other, mostly Western states, to hinder India's technological development.

Indeed, four decades ago, nuclear technology-holding countries formed the NSG in direct response to India having detonated a nuclear explosive device. After having thereafter seeking to blunt India's nuclear development for a quarter century, beginning in the 2000s, India's emergence as a high-growth country with sensitive nuclear technology (SNT), including nuclear weapons and global strategic aspirations led the NSG to reconsider its relationship with India. Pressed forward by the USA, in 2008, the NSG lifted its nuclear trade embargo against India and since 2011; it has actively considered admitting India as a member.[19]

In recent years, India has come to view non-proliferation and trade controls in a more positive light. This happened because India's strategic horizons broadened to include considerations of a nuclear-armed Pakistan that permitted its strategic nuclear assets to proliferate, the threat from terrorists aiming to possess weapons of mass destruction, a more intensive rivalry with China, and closer ties with the West. But the extent of India's departure from time-honoured positions has not been made clear by India because it has not openly articulated a detailed narrative to explain why it seeks NSG membership.[20]

In fact, India has two different kinds of rationales. One flows from India's rising aspirations for its civilian nuclear power program. The other derives from India's quest for greater international status, including nuclear status. Some Indians acknowledge that prestige matters in Indian thinking about the NSG, but so long as India is not prepared to openly link the possession of SNT and nuclear arms with international power and status, India will explain its interest in NSG membership instead by focusing on more limited, tangible, and utilitarian grounds.[21]

These include India's desire to participate in rule-making about nuclear commerce, as distinct from India's current status outside the NSG as a rule-taker. The value of membership has been underlined to New Delhi through its pursuit of another NSG-related interest: to import SNT from suppliers. The NSG guidelines require that recipients of SNT be NPT parties. France in this decade therefore denied a request by India to supply it items for uranium enrichment. If admitted to the NSG,

India will aim to rescind that consensus rule.[22] India needs to involve itself more in the realm of the nuclear power and energy cooperation regime. One of the achievements of New Delhi has been the involvement of India in the creation of a weapon-free world regime on the lines of the Atoms for Peace approach.

The Manohar Parrikar Research Institute reports that " In the pre-2005 period, the Indian government as well as most Indian analysts had approached the four export control regimes – the Nuclear Suppliers Group (NSG), the Missile Technology Control Regime (MTCR), the Wassenaar Arrangement (WA) and the Australia group (AG) – with suspicion. Such an approach was not unnatural considering the fact that the first two, namely, the NSG and the MTCR, had actively worked against Indian interests. The NSG denied fuel for the Tarapur Atomic Power Station (TAPS) while the USA used MTCR provisions to prevent the transfer of cryogenic engine technology – a purely civilian space technology – by Russia to India thereby setting back the Indian space programme by more than a decade." The NSG was primarily set up to counter the twilight zone nations such as India that had detonated their nuclear options, India being in 1974 part of Operation Shakti. The NSG created have and have-not flocks in the nuclear sphere of the nations. Thus, India too did not join any of the CD (Conference on Disarmament) and the CTBT (Comprehensive Test Ban Treaty). India was dubbed by nations such as the USA as nuclear pariahs and thus India, Israel and the Islamic Republic of Pakistan came to be called nuclear have-nots which was foiled by both New Delhi and Islamabad testing their nuclear options.

The author writes that, "With the conclusion of the India-US nuclear cooperation agreements after July 2005 and the September 2008 NSG exemption for India from some of the restrictive provisions of the Group's guidelines, the Indian attitude and approach to these regimes turned favourable. India began to positively consider the possibility of becoming a member of all these regimes. This attitude was further reinforced by the November 2010 joint statement issued during President Barack Obama's visit to India, which explicitly endorsed India's candidature for the four multilateral export control regimes. India had then considered NSG membership as being the most important. The US 'Food for Thought' paper on the question of India's membership circulated to NSG members for their consideration and feedback just prior to the June 2011 Consultative Group (CG) and plenary meeting in Noordwijk, the Netherlands, further vetted India's aspirations."[23]

Even though all NSG plenaries from 2011 onwards continued to discuss 'NSG('s) relationship with India' (in the words of NSG communiqués), there was very little forward movement. To a certain extent, the delay could be attributed to India as well. For one, India had not even applied for NSG membership until May 2016, that is, just prior to the 2016 Seoul plenary. Nor could it have because one of the important requirements for applying for the Group's membership, leave alone being actually admitted, was that an applicant state should be a NSG adherent.[24]

The author further asserts that "It is true that as part of its commitments to the NSG for obtaining the September 2008 exemption, India had addressed a communication to the IAEA Director-General stating that "India has adhered to the Guidelines and Annexes of the Nuclear Suppliers group". But this was not in line with the actual NSG requirement that, for recognition as an NSG adherent, the adherence letter to the IAEA Director-General must also include a statement to the effect that the adherence communication be published as an IAEA Information Circular (INFCIRC). India sent such a communication to the IAEA only on 9 May 2016, just before formally applying to the NSG for membership on the next day. (It is, of course, altogether another matter that the then US President sent to the US Congress in October 2008 a false certification to the effect that "the USA assesses that India has adhered to the guidelines and annexes of the NSG and the MTCR, and has done so in a manner consistent with the procedures and/or practices of those regimes."[25]

The IDSA paper further reiterates that "Pakistan followed India's footsteps about a week later by sending to the IAEA Director-General an NSG adherence communication on 18 May 2016 and subsequently on the very next day a letter to the NSG Chair applying for membership in the grouping. Both India's and Pakistan's applications were sent well ahead of the June 23-24, 2016, Seoul NSG Plenary. Given the special nature of the applications, the first by non-NPT states and that too by states possessing nuclear weapons, the then Chair of the NSG, Ambassador Rafael Grossi of Argentina, had recommended an extraordinary plenary session to discuss the special characteristics of the applications prior to the regular plenary session."[26]

The White House press release, in the aftermath of the 24 June 2023 joint statement contends that "President Biden and Prime Minister Modi underscored the important role nuclear energy plays in global decarbonisation efforts and affirmed nuclear energy as a necessary resource to meet our nations' climate, energy transition, and energy security needs. The leaders noted ongoing negotiations between the Nuclear Power Corporation of India Limited (NPCIL) and Westinghouse Electric Company (WEC) for the construction of six nuclear reactors in India."[27] Under PM Modi, India has always stressed that Nuclear power for New Delhi is for deterrence and peaceful purposes and India has also adopted the No First Use approach to deter the international community from tarnishing India's image as a war monger and a hegemon which New Delhi has never been.

"They welcomed intensified consultations between the US DOE and India's DAE for facilitating opportunities for WEC to develop a techno-commercial offer for the Kovvada nuclear project. They also noted the ongoing discussion on developing next generation small modular reactor technologies in a collaborative mode for the domestic market as well as for export. The USA reaffirms its support for India's membership in the Nuclear Suppliers Group and commits to continue engagement with likeminded partners to advance this goal."[28] Thus, under Prime Minister Narendra Modi, both the nations have come a long way ahead from the fracas over CTBT, NPT and CD. Now, under Modian leadership, the Indian nuclear isolation has ended due to deft carrying out of canny nuclear diplomacy with astute interfacing and networking with the comity of nations.

The prestigious portal, 'Nuclear Engineering Internationale' reported that "The USA reaffirmed its support for Indian membership of the Nuclear Suppliers Group (NSG) during a state visit to Washington by Prime Minister Narendra Modi. A joint statement by Modi and US President Joe Biden covered a wide range of subjects, with nuclear mentioned only in one para (number 22)". It said: "Prime Minister Modi underscored the important role nuclear energy plays in global decarbonisation efforts and affirmed nuclear energy as a necessary resource to meet our nations' climate, energy transition, and energy security needs."[29]

The leaders noted ongoing negotiations between the Nuclear Power Corporation of India Limited (NPCIL) and Westinghouse Electric Company (WEC) for the construction of six nuclear reactors in India. They welcomed intensified consultations between the US Department of Energy (DOE) and India's Department of Atomic Energy (DAE) "for facilitating opportunities for WEC to develop a techno-commercial offer for the Kovvada nuclear project". They also noted the ongoing discussion on developing next generation small modular reactor technologies in a collaborative mode for the domestic market as well as for export. Finally, "the USA reaffirms its support for India's membership in the Nuclear Suppliers Group and commits to continue engagement with like-minded partners to advance this goal."[30] What the New Delhi dispensation and Prime Minister Modi have been stating repeatedly from rostrums in India and abroad in the context of the international institutions and bilateral trysts is that India has developed its nuclear potential for peaceful measures and global and bilateral nuclear energy cooperation where the renewables and the unconventional forms of energy cooperation can take place and materialise, thus clarifying the adversarial claims that New Delhi can go beyond mere energy cooperation and further weaponise its nuclear capability.

The portal further reports that "In March 2019, India and the USA issued a joint statement agreeing to strengthen security and civil nuclear cooperation, including the construction of six US nuclear power units. This followed a visit to India by Andrea Thompson, the US

Undersecretary of State for arms control and international security."[31] In the past, the 123 civil nuclear cooperation agreement was signed after a lot of hectoring by the US Congress and the then American President, George Bush, stood fast to the White House's intent to galvanise support for the 123 waiver in the 1954 Atomic Energy Act where some exceptions can be inserted to supply nuclear knowhow to nations such as India, even if they have detonated their nuclear options.

Prime Minister Modi pitched for India's membership in the Nuclear Supplier's Group in May 2019. *WION* reports that "Prime Minister Narendra Modi on Wednesday pitched for India's inclusion in the Nuclear Suppliers Group (NSG) saying that the country faces a challenge in nuclear energy because it is not a member of the group of nuclear supplier countries and faces issue of supply of fuel. The Prime Minister made the remarks during an interaction session at the Bloomberg Global Business Forum here."[32]

WION further reports that "We have the challenge of nuclear energy because we are not a member of NSG (Nuclear Suppliers Group), so we face the issue of supply of fuel. If we get a solution on that front, then we can come out as a model and work in this sector. The Prime Minister said he had set a new target due to progress achieved so far. India had earlier set a target to achieve 175 gig watt of renewable energy. I am happy we are way ahead of the time. We have already achieved the work of 120 gig watt. While I was speaking in the UN yesterday, I have set a new target of 450 gig watt of renewable energy," he said answering a question on renewable energy. Modi had raised the issue of India's membership of NSG with UN Secretary-General Antonio Guterres during their meeting on the sidelines of the G7 summit last month. He had said that India is moving towards clean energy including investment-intensive nuclear power for which NSG membership is crucial to building investor confidence."[33] Thus, public diplomacy as a negotiation tool along with summitry at the G7 has been utilised deftly by PM Narendra Modi in a bid to bolster the transactions of India at the nuclear energy high table. The stress on India being a peacenik nuclear country has emerged as the key foundation stone to becoming a member of the NSG akin to the Indian candidature for the coveted seat at the United Nations Security Council.

In January 2003, the Cabinet Committee on Security (CCS) led by the then Prime Minister A.B. Vajpayee outlined an overview of India's nuclear doctrine. Some of these key tenets are "the building and maintenance of a credible minimum deterrent, a posture of 'no first use (NFU)', nuclear weapons will only be used in retaliation against a nuclear attack on Indian territory or on Indian forces anywhere.[34] Nuclear retaliation to a first strike will be massive and designed to inflict unacceptable damage, non-use of nuclear weapons against non-nuclear weapon states" (MEA, GoI, 2003, p. 1). But, there was a major change in the subsequent years. Shivshankar Menon, the then national security advisor, during a speech in 2010 dubbed the nuclear doctrine of India as "no first use against non-nuclear weapon states". It means that nuclear weapons may be used first against another nuclear state (Menon, 2010; Jaishankar, 2017). However, such words were not heard again and it seemed merely a momentary signal against India's opponents. But over the last few years, there has been speculation that the Modi government may reconsider nuclear doctrine and strategy. A few incidents gave rise to that speculation.[35]

The BJP election manifesto 2014 for the Lok Sabha polls pointed out that the party would like to "study in detail India's nuclear doctrine, and revise and update it, to make it relevant to challenges of current times [and] maintain a credible minimum deterrent that is in tune with changing geostatic realities" (BJP Election Manifesto 2014, p. 39). The use of words like 'revision' and 'upgrading' of nuclear doctrine in the election manifesto have led some analysts to conclude that India is likely to abandon the policy of 'no first use'.[36] However, the doubt was soon cleared. Narendra Modi, who was the BJP's prime ministerial candidate at that time, stated in an interview that "no first use is a very good initiative of [Vajpayee] and there is no compromise on this. We are very clear on this" (*NewsX*, 2014; Jaishankar, 2017).[37] But another speculation also aroused when India's former Defence Minister Manohar Parrikar, sparked controversy by stating that "Why lot of people say that India has 'no first use' policy, Why should I bind myself to a…I should say I am a responsible nuclear power and I will not use it irresponsibly. This is my thinking. Some of them may immediately tomorrow flash that Parrikar says that nuclear doctrine has changed. It has not changed in any government policy but my concept" (Singh, 2016, p. 1).[38]

However, he later clarified that the government policy had not changed and it was his personal opinion on the matter. Similarly, in August 2019, India's current Defence Minister Rajnath Singh, speaking at a ceremony in Pokhran gave rise to discussion on the doctrine of 'no-first-use', where he stated that "Till today, our nuclear policy is 'no first use'. What happens in future depends on the circumstances" (Roche, 2019, p. 1).[39] It is noteworthy here that these remarks were made in the heat of exacerbated tensions in Indo-Pak relations due to scrapping of Article 370 and the subsequent split of Jammu and Kashmir into two Union territories by the Central Government.[40] There have been a slew of deliberations and discussions which have been going on since the relentless use of cross-border terrorism as an instrument of external relations in the context of India-Pakistan relations. All in all, the theme of 'No First Use' has cropped up again and again and may serve as a galvanising argument and a significant attendant factor as far as the India's nuclear doctrine goes.

It has been more than two decades since India had become a nuclear power in 1998. In democracies, consecutive governments often change the policy of previous governments. But there are some established areas where the broad consensus prohibits any radical shift. India's nuclear doctrine is also one such area where successive governments have maintained a continuous, conservative approach. There may be a shift in the technical requirement of the programme, for example, the pace of the programme usually depends upon the personal character of a leader, but overall, the nuclear policy has not changed irrespective of whichever party is in power whether the Congress or the BJP (Sethi, 2017).[41] Even during the first term of the Modi government, there was much speculation about a shift in nuclear policy, but a broad-based consensus demonstrated a continuous validation of nuclear doctrine.

Compared to other global nuclear powers, according to *Mukt Shabd Journal,* volume IX, issue XII, December/2020 ISSN no. 2347-3150, page 49 India's nuclear weapons are fewer than that of North Korea. However, this has helped the country to maintain basic minimum credible deterrence while minimizing nuclear escalation risk. Since India has maintained secrecy about its nuclear weapons, the ambiguity arising from the contradictory statements given by political leaders regarding nuclear policy has made some analysts to speculate on it (Jaishankar, 2017).[42] Against this backdrop, we seek to find out whether there really has been a change in India's current nuclear strategy. The analysis has been made in two broad sections. First, India's nuclear doctrine has been examined with special reference to the BJP election manifesto of 2014 for the Lok Sabha polls and second, the government response to the 2016 Uri and 2019 Pulwama attacks; both have been studied.

Rajesh Rajagopalan writes the final word and as part of a legitimate commentary on Modiji's nuclear policy since coming to power in May 2014. He writes that "India's nuclear policy has remained far steadier under the Modi government than initial rhetoric from his party suggested or what many observers feared. In this essay, three aspects of India's nuclear policy under the Modi government are examined: India's nuclear arsenal, its nuclear doctrine, and its nuclear diplomacy. Each of them shows that Indian policy has continued to develop along the same axis as the preceding governments. India's nuclear armoury has increased, but gradually, and there is little indication that India is on the cusp of any nuclear doctrinal change, especially regarding its No First Use policy. India's diplomacy has also largely continued along the same path as before, emphasizing India's membership of key multilateral arrangements from which India had been excluded, and traditional slogans such as nuclear disarmament and de-alerting of nuclear forces. Moreover, there is no indication this will change in the immediate future."[43] What is required is a sturdier pathway for India's nuclear doctrine wherein probable but very crucial amendments can be attempted and striven at and Prime Minister Modi seems to be the best bet for us as we enter a new phase of international politics which is more violent, anarchic and replete with strategic incertitude. Also, with responsible nations of the order of Russia led by Vladimir Putin going ahead with a nuclear blackmail of the West and NATO forces backing Ukraine, it has become essential for New Delhi to revise its nuclear doctrine and attendant policy.

The Economic Times reports pithily that "India's largest power producer is looking to develop another massive nuclear project just weeks after announcing its entry into the sector, a sign that Prime Minister Narendra Modi's expansion into atomic energy is gaining momentum. A venture between NTPC Ltd., which relies mostly on coal to supply energy to the world's fastest-growing population, and India's monopoly nuclear developer is in advanced talks with the government to develop two 700-megawatt reactors."[44] *The Economic Times* further reports that "Modi is aiming to more than triple India's nuclear fleet over the next decade to expand the share of electricity from cleaner sources, as the nation seeks to zero out carbon emissions by 2070. The country currently generates about 70 per cent of its electricity using coal and around 3 per cent from nuclear, and has opened its atomic industry to state-controlled firms beyond the Nuclear Power Corp. of India Ltd. in a bid to speed adoption of nuclear energy."[45] Thus, instead of harping on the nuclear power strength of India, New Delhi is going ahead with the image making exercise of India as being a peacenik and peace-making nation which sees only trade and commercial prospects in the larger nuclear energy trade firmament.

India has been gaining in strength and prestige despite its nuclear pelf and strength as the global community is reciprocating the Indian nuclear rationale. An IAEA report notes that "IAEA Director-General Rafael Mariano Grossi met Prime Minister Narendra Modi in New Delhi on Monday as part of his four-day visit to India. The two leaders discussed ways to foster India-IAEA ties across diverse sectors. 'India's civil nuclear programme is key for its decarbonisation. Prime Minister Modi and I agreed on the importance of financing and technology access, placing nuclear at the forefront of global solutions,' Mr. Grossi said. The leaders will 'intensify cooperation' ahead of the United Nations Climate Change Conference (COP 28) in the United Arab Emirates and next year's Nuclear Energy Summit in Belgium, Mr. Grossi added."[46] Though the manner in which the International Atomic Energy Agency investigated Iraq at the behest of the West and the USA to indict Baghdad and Saddam Hussein as being holders of weapons of mass destruction and haranguing Iraq with penalties does not run well for the IAEA which is supposed to be a neutral and impartial ombudsman in the sphere of nuclear energy.

The IAEA report further stresses that "Prime Minister Modi said that the 'fruitful discussion' with Director-General Grossi, explored avenues for expanding the role of nuclear energy to meet [India's] net zero commitment, and extending nuclear technology applications in areas like food, health, water treatment and countering plastic pollution in the global arena. In a meeting with Subrahmanyam Jaishankar, Minister of External Affairs of the Government of India, Mr. Jaishankar reiterated that 'India will always be a strong and reliable partner of IAEA.' India has 19 nuclear reactors producing about 3 per cent of its electricity. With an additional eight reactors under construction and more planned, India is currently the world's second-largest domestic builder of nuclear power plants. India's three-stage nuclear power programme builds towards using the country's abundant thorium reserves. India's approach comes with a potentially global increase in the abundance of energy resource and is being closely watched, so is India's transition to a greener economy."[47]

The report further stresses that "A member-state since 1957, India collaborates with the IAEA through various means, such as contributing to key programmes like the Nuclear Harmonization and Standardization Initiative to advance the harmonization and standardization of small modular reactor (SMR) design, construction, regulatory and industrial approaches. The Director-General aims to strengthen this and other collaborations with the country to draw benefit from India's scientific and institutional capacities."[48]

> ... One may also delve into the rubric, nature and content of India's nuclear doctrine. The text is given verbatim, "India's nuclear doctrine can be summarized as follows:

i. Building and maintaining a credible minimum deterrent;
ii. A posture of 'No First Use'; nuclear weapons will only be used in retaliation against a nuclear attack on Indian territory or on Indian forces anywhere;
iii. Nuclear retaliation to a first strike will be massive and designed to inflict unacceptable damage;
iv. Nuclear retaliatory attacks can only be authorised by the civilian political leadership through the Nuclear Command Authority;
v. Non-use of nuclear weapons against non-nuclear weapon states;
vi. However, in the event of a major attack against India, or Indian forces anywhere, by biological or chemical weapons, India will retain the option of retaliating with nuclear weapons;
vii. A continuance of strict controls on export of nuclear and missile related materials and technologies, participation in the Fissile Material Cutoff Treaty negotiations, and continued observance of the moratorium on nuclear tests;
viii. Continued commitment to the goal of a nuclear weapon-free world, through global, verifiable and non-discriminatory nuclear disarmament.[49]

3. The Nuclear Command Authority comprises a political council and an executive council. The political council is chaired by the Prime Minister. It is the sole body that can authorize the use of nuclear weapons.

4. The executive council is chaired by the National Security Advisor. It provides inputs for decision making by the Nuclear Command Authority and executes the directives given to it by the political council.

5. The CCS reviewed the existing command and control structures, the state of readiness, the targeting strategy for a retaliatory attack, and operating procedures for various stages

of alert and launch. The committee expressed satisfaction with the overall preparedness. The CCS approved the appointment of a commander-in-chief, Strategic Forces Command, to manage and administer all strategic forces.[50]

6. The CCS also reviewed and approved the arrangements for alternate chains of command for retaliatory nuclear strikes in all eventualities."[51]

Thus, a whole superstructure exists inclusive of the heads of services, the National Security Advisor and ministers in order to respond to a national security challenge in any given time and space in response to adversarial moves. The idioms of NFU, that is no 'No first use' along with the principles of the sea, land and air-based triads and with a robust command and control structure and deterrence being the fulcrum of the doctrine, the nuclear doctrine is a robust and well thought out and methodological way out and a measure to defend the nation in the case of a nonconventional aggression or security/collateral threat. The debate is out on the nullification of the 'No First Use' element in the Indian draft doctrine which kind of delimits the aggression and functionality of the nuclear power and strength of the nation. Still, lest it be forgotten that New Delhi also defines India's nuclear posture within the confines of a non-aggressive and nuclear energy cooperation strategy which does not lend too much of teeth to our draft nuclear doctrine.

Gagan Hitkari writes in *Modern Diplomacy*: "Over the years, a number of criticisms have been levied against the 'No First Use' policy. Instead, various strategists have favoured a policy of 'first use' of nuclear weapons arguing that 'No First Use' of nuclear weapons restricts action and leads to a loss of initiative by allowing the adversary to use its nuclear weapons first in combat. Other arguments bemoan the NFU as idealist and pacifist in nature, claiming that a country engaged in combat cannot rely on the passivity that stems from it. A policy of 'First Use' might be prudent in the case of conventional weapons but this does not hold true for nuclear weapons. A first strike must ensure neutralising all the nuclear capabilities of the adversary as a potential retaliatory strike has the capability of causing irreversible and unprecedented devastation due to the nature of the nuclear bomb."[52]

Gagan Hitkari further writes that "Hence, a policy of first strike is only effective when a country can ensure that its adversary lacks secure second-strike capabilities once the strike has been carried out. Although by employing NFU, the initiative to act rests with the adversary, the calculation of a first strike cannot be limited to just the first strike damage. Due to the modernisation of nuclear arsenals and development of secure second-strike capabilities, the inevitable retaliation leading from a first strike must be taken into account. Therefore, even an elaborate offensive strategy cannot assure victory or help escape the extent of the damage."[53]

The author further stresses that "First use of nuclear weapons is mostly advocated in cases where the adversary's preparation for a nuclear strike is known. It is argued that in such a scenario, it is in the benefit of nations to use nuclear weapons rather than potentially losing them to a neutralising strike. Although possibilities of a first strike can be known, this information does not guarantee the certainty of a nuclear strike. In modern times, states use nuclear weapons not as an end but as a means for achieving their ends through coercive diplomacy and nuclear brinkmanship. In such a scenario, even stationing of nuclear weapons in an aggressive position cannot be taken as certainty of a nuclear strike. Hence, if a state indulges in a preventive strike, it will be regarded as an act of aggression leading to potentially devastating retaliatory strikes as well as widespread condemnation."[54]

Why No First Use?

India has for long presented itself as a responsible nuclear power. In the aftermath of Pokhran-II, India faced widespread criticism and international sanctions on what was regarded as an act of unprovoked aggression. In order to escape this predicament, India found official adoption of NFU to be the most prudent way forward. NFU helped in representing India as a responsible nuclear power by relegating nuclear weapons to purely defensive purposes. A more important imperative for NFU is its strategic viability. A policy of 'first use' advocates for forces to be on hair-trigger alert leading to a potential arms race which in turn contributes to instability and crisis. A 'first use' policy can also lead to threats of miscalculation, increasing the risk of an accidental launch. NFU, on the other hand, provides a relatively relaxed posture which in turn helps in avoiding a costly and potentially devastating arms race. An abandonment of NFU will likely have repercussions in India's immediate neighbourhood. The policy of 'No first use' has been central to Indian strategic thinking since the Nehruvian era. The policy against use of nuclear weapons can be traced back to the 1950s when Prime Minister Nehru called for a standstill agreement proposing a ban on nuclear testing. In 1965, India advocated for a strong non-discriminatory treaty imposing a ban on nuclear weapons. Hence, the strategic culture of nuclear minimalism and restraint showed itself into the adoption of the 'No first use' policy. A shift in this policy has the potential of further aggravating hostilities in India's neighbourhood.

The policy of 'No first use' of nuclear weapons and the nuclear minimalism of India's nuclear doctrine has solidified its image as a strong, credible and morally responsible nuclear power. NFU offers India great leverage in the international community. India's bid for membership of the Nuclear Suppliers Group also relies on its image as a responsible nuclear power.[55]

At a time when countries are actively advocating for the realisation of a stronger non-proliferation regime, India should be at the forefront of facilitating that end rather than taking a belligerent stance and abandoning the crucial diplomatic leverage it enjoys in the international community. Although it is important to re-evaluate India's doctrinal position to ensure that national security is not compromised, the abandonment of NFU does not present any benefits to this end. India should continue with the longstanding NFU and actively work towards the realisation of a stronger, more equal non-proliferation regime.

NOTES

1. President Dwight Eisenhower. 'Atoms for Peace Programme,' URL https:// www.eisenhowerlibrary.gov/research/online-documents/atoms-peace#:~:text=In%20his%20Atoms%20for%20Peace,into%20a%20benefit%20for%20mankind (Online Web), accessed on 10 December 2023.
2. Ibid.
3. News clipping, *Washington Post*. 'Eisenhower Pushes Operation Candor,' 21 September 1953, Charles Masterson Papers, Box 1, Operation Candor; NAID #12022743.

4. Atoms for Peace Draft [C. D. Jackson Papers, Box 30, 'Atoms for Peace – Evolution (5)'; NAID #12021574.
5. Nehru on Disarmament, URL https://meaindia.nic.in/cdgeneva/?pdf0596?000, (Online Web), accessed on 10 December, 2023.
6. Ibid.
7. Ibid., Fn. 1.
8. Ibid., Fn. 2
9. United Nations. 'Peace, Dignity and the Health of the Planet,' URL https://www.un.org/en/about-us/un-charter/chapter-1 (Online Web), accessed on 8 December 2023.
10. Ibid., Fn. 1.
11. Ibid, Fn. 2.
12. Ibid, Fn. 3.
13. Ibid., 4.
14. Ibid., 5.
15. About the Nuclear Suppliers Group, URL https://www.nuclearsuppliersgroup.org/en/about-nsg (Online Web), accessed on 1 December, 2023.
16. Ibid.
17. Ibid., Fn. 1.
18. Srinivas Laxman. 'US reiterates support for India's Membership of NSG,' *The Times of India*, 24 July 2023.
19. Mark Hibbs. 'India's Pursuit of membership in the Nuclear Supplier's Group,' Carnegie Endowment for Peace, URL https://carnegieendowment.org/2018/02/13/eyes-on-prize-india-s-pursuit-of-membership-in-nuclear-suppliers-group-pub-75535 (Online Web), accessed on 1 November 2023.
20. Ibid.
21. Ibid.
22. Ibid.
23. Ibid.
24. IDSA Comments: G. Balachandran. 'India and the Nuclear Suppliers Group,' URL https://www.idsa.in/issuebrief/india-and-the-nsg-membership_gbalachandran_051016 (Online Web), accessed on 1 May 2023.
25. Ibid.
26. Ibid.
27. White House release on joint statement of the Indian PM Narendra Modi and President Joe Biden, URL https://www.whitehouse.gov/briefing-room/statements-releases/2023/06/22/joint-statement-from-the-united-states-and-india/ (Online Web), accessed on 1 October 2023.
28. Ibid.
29. Nuclear Engineering International. 'US Supports India's bid for the Nuclear Supplier's Group,' URL https://www.neimagazine.com/news/newsus-reaffirms-support-for-indian-membership-of-nuclear-suppliers-group-10967702 (Online Web), accessed on 1 November 2023.
30. Ibid.
31. Ibid., Fn.1.
32. 'PM Modi pitches for India's membership of the Nuclear Supplier's Group,' URL https://www.wionews.com/india-news/pm-narendra-modi-pitches-for-indias-

membership-of-nuclear-suppliers-group-252049 (Online Web), accessed on 1 October 2023.

33. Ibid.
34. BJP Election Manifesto (2014). Ek Bharat – Shreshtha Bharat. New Delhi: Bharatiya Janata Party. Retrieved 12 February 2019, from http://www.bjp.org/images/pdf_2014/full_manifesto_english_07.04.2014.pdf
35. Dalton, T. & Perkovich, G. (2016, 1 June). India's Nuclear Options and Escalation Dominance. Washington: Carnegie Endowment for International Peace, retrieved 12 March 2019 from *The Wire*: https://carnegieendowment.org/files/CP_273_India_Nuclear_Final.pdf
36. *NewsX*. (2014, 16 April). 70 Mins of Modi: Watch Narendra Modi's most wide-ranging interview. (Video file). Retrieved 23 February 23, 2019, from https://www.youtube.com/watch?v=lTlOPpknMdo
37. *NewsX*. (2014, 16 April). 70 Mins of Modi: Watch Narendra Modi's most wide-ranging interview. (Video file). Retrieved 23 February 2019, from https://www.youtube.com/watch?v=lTlOPpknMdo
38. Singh, S., Miglani, S., & Chalmers, J. (2014, 7 April). BJP puts 'no first use' nuclear policy in doubt. Retrieved 25 February 2019, from Reuters: https://in.reuters.com/article/india-election-bjp-manifestoidINDEEA3605820140407. (2016, 11 November). Manohar Parrikar questions India's no-first-use nuclear policy, adds 'my thinking', *The Indian Express*, Retrieved 12 March 2019 from https://indianexpress.com/article/india/india-news-india/manohar-parrikar-questions-no-firstuse-nuclear-policy-adds-my-thinking-4369062/
39. Singh, S. (2016, 11 November). Manohar Parrikar questions India's no-first-use nuclear policy, adds 'my thinking'. *The Indian Express*, retrieved 12 March 2019 from https://indianexpress.com/article/india/india-news-india/manohar-parrikar-questions-no-firstuse-nuclear-policy-adds-my-thinking-4369062/
40. Roche, E. (2019, 16 August. Rajnath Singh sparks debate on no-first-use nuclear doctrine, retrieved 15 December 2019 from *Mint* https://www.livemint.com/news/india/rajnath-singh-sparksdebate-on-no-first-use-nuclear-doctrine-1565978545173.html
41. Sethi, M. (2017, 19 June). Three Years of the Modi Government: Indian Nuclear Policy and Diplomacy, retrieved 17 February 2019 from Institute of Peace and Conflict Studies: http://www.ipcs.org/comm_select.php?articleNo=5300
42. D. Jaishankar. 'Decoding India's Nuclear Status,' *The Wire*, January 2017.
43. C. Rajagopalan. 'Modi Sticks to India's Nuclear path,' *International Politics,* June 2021.
44. *The Economic Times*, 22 January 2022.
45. Ibid.
46. Ilinaz Kabalci. 'India and International Atomic Energy Agency,' URL https://www.iaea.org/newscenter/news/iaea-chief-meets-prime-minister-modi-fostering-india-iaea-ties-across-diverse-sectors (Online Web), accessed on 1 October 2023.
47. Ibid.
48. Ibid., Fn. 1.
49. 'India's Draft Nuclear Doctrine,' URL https://archive.pib.gov.in/archive/releases98/lyr2003/rjan2003/04012003/r040120033.html (Online Web), accessed on 10 May 2023.

50. Ibid.
51. Ibid., Fn. 1.
52. Gagan Hitkari. 'India's NFU Policy,' URL https://moderndiplomacy.eu/2023/01/18/why-indias-no-first-use-policy-must-remain/ (Online Web), accessed on 1 November 2023.
53. Ibid.
54. Ibid., Fn. 1.
55. Ibid.

Chapter Eight

India and the IPR Ecosystem

Intellectual Property Rights have been the pet palaver since long in India and the world over. The consequential IPR regime too has been a concomitant product with the IPR concept and actuality and the regime, the world over. It has been an effort since Nehruvian times that there ought to be a strengthening of the patent holders wherein the inventers of the product concerned or the process under consideration can become the staple fare order of the day, technically speaking. Monopoly of knowledge systems and inventions ought to remain prominent as the inventers and innovators who have blazed a trail of glory need to be protected and compensated for their endeavours in the national and societal interests which are not different in nature and purpose and principle.

The ideal objective of the policy is to enumerate methodologies of socio-economic development in a manner which facilitates the nom de plume of localized commerce, trade and primarily would have led to the protection of local industry. Opening up India for the greater and larger multinationals when Indian industry was just finding its feet could have led to the idiom of the ruin of the Indian industry and innovation and scientific development and progression. This was true in the Nehruvian times. Critics of Prime Minister Modi's IPR policy have a few illogical ruses to raise which can be enumerated as follows.

The author contends that "The policy in no way shows how it will be able to ensure the socio-cultural development of India. The data shows that if India had opted for early TRIPS implementation, the market power of foreign firms would have been greater and the people would have suffered the drawbacks of the strong intellectual property regime. Furthermore, India supplies a number of pharmaceuticals to the USA and the European market, and it is ironic that the policy would give a little more than lip service to India in case of generic pharmaceuticals. The policy focuses on improving the IPR output at various universities, laboratories and other institutions but it does not look at the Council of Scientific and Industrial Research laboratories which have failed to yield patents that could earn revenue for the CSIR. As suggested by the national IP policy the connection of universities and institutions with the IP laboratory is next to nil."[1]

The policy considers IP rights as an economic tool whereas it is a regulatory tool for the government and it should not use it as an incentive.[2] The policy should be guided by a contract between society and the state on the basis of its consequences for the development process. Incentives should be awarded only by asking as to which kind of innovation is being offered by a particular system of rewards. The policy seeks to promote open source drug discovery but it fails to announce open source licensing which is law-favouring. The policy states that IP education should be given in all schools and universities and proposes awareness programmes but the greatest concern is that awareness on an IP maximalist agenda will destroy the balance between IP and public interest which the courts have tried to maintain.[3]

Recently, the Union Cabinet approved the Modi Government's Intellectual Property Rights Policy which is clearly based on the pro-IP ideology. The national intellectual property policy is the first of its kind drafted for India and rewards big capital. The policy deals with all types of intellectual property together in one structure and aims at encouraging intellectual property owners by sanctioning them monopoly rights. The policy aims at governing the Trade Marks, Patents and Designs Act which was controlled by the Controller-General of Patents, Designs and Trade Marks, the Copyright Act which is administered by the Ministry of Human Resources and Development, the Semiconductor Integrated Circuits Layout-Design Act controlled by the Information Technology

Department, the Biological Diversity Act which was under the Ministry of Environment and Forests and the Protection of Plant Varieties and Farmers' Rights Act which is under the aegis of the Ministry of Agriculture. The very purpose of the national intellectual property is to create awareness about the need for intellectual property rights as an economic tool and a marketable financial asset. Here, the policy-makers should be reminded of how the public banking system was robbed when it relied on the valuation of Kingfisher to release funds to Vijay Mallya. Such a policy will enable inventors to ascertain their ability for protecting and generating intellectual property rights and thereby help in strengthening the IP culture which in turn will generate employment opportunities and help to create wealth in the economy. The tough measures which have been taken by the government in the last two decades have led to the establishment of a TRIPS agreement and a dynamic IPR regime. Furthermore, India was the first country to ratify the Marrakesh Treaty 2013, for access to published works by visually-impaired persons. The accession to the Madrid Protocol in 2013 is a move towards global alignment for proprietors of marks.

Ayushi Gupta writes that "The courts in India have lucidly expressed the purpose of our laws by regularly enforcing IPRs through judicial pronouncements. The intellectual property in India is regulated by various rules and regulations and the legal provisions should be implemented in a way so as to avoid any kind of conflict. Issues relating to technical, economic, and legal should be resolved by consensus as they are for the benefit of the public at large. The mission and vision of the new IP Policy Intellectual Property promotes culture, science and technology, traditional knowledge and biodiversity resources. Knowledge is the main component of development and knowledge owned is transformed into knowledge shared. This policy aims to bring about a balanced intellectual property rights system in India in order to stimulate creativity and innovation, accelerate security of food, and protect the environment."[4] The objectives of the new IPR Policy are (1) Awareness of IPR. Earlier, monetisation of knowledge was never a tradition in India but our age is driven by the knowledge economy and hence there arises a need to propagate the value of transforming knowledge into IP assets. A number of IP inventors and creators are unaware of the benefits of IP rights. This policy adopts a slogan of Creative India: Innovative India and suggests linking it with other national initiatives like 'Make in India', 'Smart Cities', etc."

Ayushi Gupta further suggests that "It is also suggested to set up a 'Hall of Fame' to celebrate the success of IP innovators and distribution of awards, World IP Day should be celebrated in different cities, an IP museum should be established, IP should be included in the courses and curriculum of educational institutions and universities, and the media should be engaged so as to educate them about the importance of IP related issues. Moving exhibits such as road shows, and IP promotion in multiple linguistics and pictorial representations for those who are unable to read should be made a part of this programme.[5] IPR generation: The number of IP filings and grants has tremendously increased in recent years in India; however, the percentage of filings by Indians remains relatively low."

The author further asserts that, "India is among the top five filers in the world with the maximum being filed by Indians. Much contribution to the Indian economy is brought from the copyright sector. Research and development needs to be promoted through various tax benefits so that affordable drugs could be developed. The digital library of traditional knowledge should be expanded beyond Unani, Ayurveda, Siddha and Yoga. This objective can be achieved by developing affordable drugs related to neglected diseases, focusing on IPR driven research, encourage innovation in agriculture and pisciculture, increasing domestic filing of patent applications and generating technologies relating to cyber security."[6]

Most of the international community along with Prime Minister Narendra Modi's utterances too have seemed to have gelled as both clamour and realize that there is a kind of old rootedness, obsoleteness and arcaneness in the manner in which the Indian IPR regime has been developed and created. Intellectual Property (IP) is related to the human brain applied for creativity and invention. Various efforts in terms of inputs of manpower, time, energy, skill, money, etc., are required to invent or create something new. As per law, legal rights or monopoly rights are given to creators or innovators to harvest the economic benefits of their inventions or creations. These intellectual property rights (IPR) are territorial rights that can be registered with a legal authority in some presentable or tangible form which can be sold or bought or licensed, similar to physical property. IPR provides a secure environment for investors, scientists, artists, designers, traders, etc., to foster innovation and scientific temper. In the present scenario of **globalization,** IPR is the focal point in global trade practices and livelihood across the world. A balanced IPR system is one of the key mechanisms to support the country's innovation and development objectives.

The IPR System in India

The origins of India's IPR system date back to British colonial rule when, as a colony, the state enacted various rules and enforcement mechanisms pertaining to IP rights. Post-independence, India retained elements of these structures while updating some guiding regulations and other bureaucratic structures. As India moved towards liberalization, privatization, and globalization in the 1990s, and later, Indian policymakers made further adjustments to keep up with the growing needs of domestic and international stakeholders. Indian IPR laws fully conform to the Agreement on Trade Related Aspects of Intellectual Property Rights under WTO aegis. IPR Policy 2016 Adopted in May 2016, the IPR Policy is a giant leap by the Government of India to spur creativity and stimulate innovation. It lays the roadmap for the future of IPRs in India.

Lok Sabha documents inform us that "The policy seeks to reinforce the IPR framework in the country that will create public awareness about economic, social and cultural benefits of IPRs among all sections of society, stimulate IPR generation and commercialization, modernize and strengthen service-oriented IPR administration (see Annexure I) as also the enforcement and adjudicatory mechanisms for combating IPR infringements. Vision Statement of the Policy" (To create) an India where creativity and innovation are stimulated by intellectual property for the benefit of all; an India where intellectual property promotes advancement in science and technology, arts and culture, traditional knowledge and biodiversity resources; an India where knowledge is the main driver of development, and knowledge owned is transformed into knowledge shared."[7] Thus, the IPR law in India runs through the modicum and instrumentality of the Patents Act of 1971 wherein creativity and innovation spawn and lead to the germination of true blue knowledge routines and healthy and sustainable traditions for the future.

The Lok Sabha documents on IPR further inform us that "The policy lays down seven objectives which are elaborated with steps to be undertaken by the identified nodal ministry/department. The objectives of the policy are: (1) IPR Awareness: Outreach and Promotion – To create public awareness about the economic, social and cultural benefits of IPRs among all sections. (2) Generation of IPRs – To stimulate the generation of IPRs: India has a large talent pool of scientific and technological talent spread over R&D institutions, enterprises, universities and technical institutes. There is a need to tap this fertile knowledge resource and stimulate the creation of IP assets. (see Annexures II and III for number of applications for patents and top patentees). (3) Legal and legislative framework – To have strong and effective IPR laws, which balance the interests of rights owners with larger public interests. (4) Administration and Management – To modernize and strengthen service-oriented IPR administration. (5) Commercialization of IPR – Get value for IPRs through commercialization. (6) Enforcement and Adjudication – To strengthen the enforcement and adjudicatory mechanisms for combating IPR infringements. (7) Human Capital Development – To strengthen and expand human resources, institutions and capacities for teaching, training, research and skill building in IPRs."[8]

The United Nations too has introduced a narrative and a set of clearly defined principles in order to set up and establish a framework for balancing out between creativity and intellectual property. How can someone, copy the Monalisa, Guernica or a Van Gogh painting? The United Nations portal informs us pithily that "UN clearly pointed out in an article published by the United Nations Development Programme that "greater effort needs to be devoted to protecting intellectual property rights. Failing to properly reward creators is holding back growth. Legal frameworks that protect the rights of creators and secure fair remuneration for them is key". Precisely, 'The Art of Protection' initiative, aims at highlighting the importance of protecting the intellectual property of creators."[9]

The United Nations project further echoes that "The project seeks to provide assistance to artists and designers through awareness and training so that they can sustain themselves with their creative work while helping to develop small businesses in the creative industry. Sustainable growth and decent work are related to respect for the work of others. When intellectual property rights are ignored, artists and designers might perceive that their own works do not have the recognition they deserve and, as a result, many of them develop or find other livelihoods."[10] Still, what one can argue is the notion that intellectual property also means a different entity altogether wherein, artists and creators specially in the sphere of handicrafts and tribally-manufactured artefacts can go ahead to delve into the collectivization of producing handicrafts and artefacts while adhering to the canon of Intellectual Property Law.

A prestigious web portal informs us about the scenario in the United Kingdom. It contends that "Intellectual property refers to creations of the mind. Having the right type of intellectual property protection can prevent others from stealing or copying your inventions and creations; such as the name, design or look of your products. It is important for businesses to be aware of the different types of intellectual property rights to ensure the ultimate protection for their creations and to maximise their competitive position within the market. Intellectual property rights are divided into two main categories (in the UK)":[11]

- **Registered rights:** Registered rights are granted on application to the UK Intellectual Property Office. With registered rights, owners can stop others from using their creations without permission. These include trademarks, patents and registered designs.

- **Unregistered rights:** Unregistered rights arise automatically and give protection on the creation of your work. These include confidential information, copyright, unregistered design rights and unregistered trademarks.

Different Types of Intellectual Property Protections include:

Copyright

Copyright protects original works of authorship such as literary, artistic, musical and dramatic works. Copyright also protects computer software, sound recordings, broadcasts, films and architecture. Essentially, it protects the expression of an idea. It does not protect against independent development of the same idea(s). Copyright arises automatically and lasts for 50 to 70 years depending on the creation or work.[12]

Patents

Patents protect new inventions and innovative technical features of products and processes. An inventor is not entitled to a patent as an automatic right, as a grant of a patent is not automatic. It is necessary to file an application for a patent in order to have this protection. Patents can provide a high level of protection for businesses that are ready to commercialise a new product.[13]

Trademark

Trademarks protect symbols, words, phrases that distinguish products or services of one party from another. Registration of a trademark is not required; however, it does confer certain advantages. It is possible to apply for a trademark in most jurisdictions. A UK-registered trademark will only be enforceable in the UK, while an EU trademark will be enforceable throughout Europe.

Design Rights

Design rights protect the appearance of a product. This can be the appearance of the whole product or part of the product. A registered design right is valid for a maximum of 25 years, which requires a registration renewal every five years. Unregistered design rights, on the other hand, will give a right against copying and under the UK design right, this protection will last for ten years from its first marketing.

Confidential Information – Trade Secrets

It is also possible to protect information that is considered to be sensitive to your business, through confidential information rights. This will cover know-how and trade secrets. These are not strictly intellectual property rights; however, they will protect sensitive information, both commercial and technical, and they do not need to be registered. We can assist you with various aspects of intellectual property rights, from identifying these rights and guiding you through the registration process."[14]

Union Minister of State (Independent Charge) for Science and Technology, MoS PMO, Department of Atomic Energy and Department of Space and MoS Personnel, Public Grievances and Pensions, Dr. Jitendra Singh has said that "Start-Ups Intellectual Property Rights Protection" is aimed at promoting innovation and entrepreneurship. In his inaugural address at the National Intellectual Property Festival, organised by the CSIR at the National Physical Laboratory in New Delhi, Dr. Jitendra Singh said the filing of Intellectual Property Rights (IPR) including Patents and Trademark by Start-Ups,[15] along with industry linkages will encourage innovation and motivate enterprise in India. Under the leadership of Prime Minister Shri Narendra Modi, after the Government came up with the IPR Act in 2016, the Trademark Registration process has come down to one month, which was more than one year earlier, he said. Soon after this, a 'Start-Ups Intellectual Property Rights Protection' scheme was brought in, which envisages 80 per cent rebate in patent filing and 40to 50 per cent rebate vis-à-vis industry and companies," the minister said.[16]

Prime Minister Narendra Modi has been prompt enough to welcome the IPR themes in the nation wherein he suggested a gathering of corporate officials and honchos that they could suggest ways out of the classical and older comprehension of the IPR regime in India. *Business India* reported that "Prime Minister Narendra Modi on Monday told a conclave of Indian and US corporate chiefs that the government is ready to accept suggestions made by a joint working group with the USA on intellectual property rights. Modi spoke at the US-India CEO Forum meeting, where US President Barack Obama and the Prime Minister jointly addressed the industry leaders of both the countries."[17]

A report published in *Livemint,* a national daily, contends that, "India's patent laws should be brought on par with global standards to make Asia's third largest economy a hub for outsourced creative services, Prime Minister Narendra Modi said on Thursday, signalling a major shift in the government's stand on the intellectual property rights (IPR) regime. "If we don't work towards bringing our intellectual property rights at par with global parameters, then the world will not keep relations with us. If we give confidence to the world on IPR, then we can become a destination globally for their creative work," Modi said, speaking at the first Global Exhibition on Services (GES), organized by the Commerce Ministry."[18]

The national daily further contended that "K.M. Gopakumar, a legal researcher with the Third World Network, a non-governmental organization, said there is only one global standard on IPR and that is TRIPS (Trade-related aspects of intellectual property rights) and India is already compliant with it. 'We are definitely not at par with the USA and EU standards. I hope the Prime Minister did not mean such standards when he said we have to be at par with global standards,' he added. Making Indian patent laws compliant with the standards of developed countries will not bring in any investment to India and will instead make it a destination for exports, which will be against the Prime Minister's Make in India initiative, said Gopakumar."[19] One aspect of the IPR regime is very palpably disconcerting wherein Indian industry and other intermediaries are not willing to equate with the standards followed in the United Kingdom and the USA. People are not ready to make the

Indian IPR regime at par with the thematic designs and functionality in the West, especially in the USA and the United Kingdom.

Pankaj Kumar writes in *SSRN*, "Economy of a country depends on various factors including its tangible and intangible assets. Intangible assets which may be a product of human ingenuity and innovation in any of the subjects like science and technology, arts and culture, traditional knowledge and biodiversity resources. Further, most intangible assets are stimulated by legal regulations and particularly Intellectual Property Rights (IPR). The power of knowledge and intellect is one of the key drivers for a nation's economic growth and socio-cultural development as it benefits the public in large. A substantial part of such knowledge is the part of free public domain which must not be claimed by a person intending to compete with others. Only new research outputs having some value addition and other products of intellect may be permitted to be monopolized by the right-holder(s)."[20]

He further writes that "Such acts of monopoly as per the law may be restricted in public interest as in the case of compulsory licensing in patented drugs. The law and the implementation framework for the IPR of a country reflect the policy of the country and national priorities, which have evolved over time, taking into account the dynamics of society development in the country and international commitments. With a view to stimulate a dynamic, vibrant and balanced intellectual property rights system in India, there is the National IPR Policy, 2016. This policy seems a major tool directing the Indian IP system in order to strengthen the Indian economy and align with related international policies. The policy addresses all facets of the IP system in the country and not only promotes IP but will nurture the IP culture to the greater level in India. The policy is expected to guide and enable innovators including creators and inventors to realize their potential for generating, protecting and utilizing IP which would contribute to wealth creation, employment opportunities and business development. It will integrate and create synergies with IP-related aspects of various sector specific policies and provide a roadmap for holistic, effective and balanced development of the IP system in India. The objectives of the policy are designed to facilitate the ease of doing business in India and attract foreign direct investment."[21]

NOTES

1. Government of India, Ministry of Commerce and Industry, Department of Industrial Policy & Promotion, National Intellectual Property Rights Policy, 5 December 2016.https://www.scconline.com/blog/post/2016/07/02/national-intellectual-property-rights-policy/
2. Swaraj Paul Barooah. India's National IPR Policy approved (Spicy IP, 13 May 2016), accessed on 9 June 2016, https://www.scconline.com/blog/post/2016/07/02/national-intellectual-property-rights-policy/
3. Dinesh Abrol. 'Who gains from the Modi Government's Intellectual Property Rights Policy' *The Wire*, 22 May 2016, accessed on 31 May 2016.
4. Ayushi Gupta. 'India's Intellectual Property Rights Regime,' URL https://www.scconline.com/blog/post/2016/07/02/national-intellectual-property-rights-policy/ (Online Web), accessed on 1 October 2023.
5. Ibid.
6. Ibid., Fn. 1.
7. Intellectual Property Rights in India, Lok Sabha Documents, URL https://loksabhadocs.nic.in/Refinput/New_Reference_Notes/English/Intellectual%20Property%20Rights%20in%20India.pdf (Online Web), accessed on 1 November 2023.
8. Ibid.
9. UN Web Portal Release. 'Promoting Intellectual Property Law to Promote Creativity,' URL https://www.un.org/en/academic-impact/promoting-intellectual-property-law-protect-creativity (Online Web), accessed on 1 October 2023.
10. Ibid.
11. 'What is Intellectual Property,' URL https://cheyneygoulding.co.uk/intellectual-property-rights-protecting-your-creativity-and-innovation/ (Online Web), accessed on 1 November 2023.
12. Ibid.
13. Ibid., Fn. 1.
14. Ibid., Fn. 2.
15. "Start Ups Intellectual Property Rights Protections," URL https://pib.gov.in/PressReleaseIframePage.aspx?PRID=1936884 (Online Web), accessed on 1 December 2023.
16. Ibid.
17. 'PM Modi ready to accept changes in the Indian IPR Law,' *Business India*, 26 January 2015.
18. 'India's IPR developments.' URL https://www.livemint.com/Politics/vW6RzcArtqHi6tUNFyoMqO/Need-to-bring-our-patent-laws-on-par-with-global-standards.html (Online Web), accessed on 1 October 2023.
19. Ibid.
20. Pankaj Kumar. 'Economics and National IPR Policy of India,' *SSRN*, 16 November 2018.
21. Ibid.

Conclusion

Regimes are important in a nation's social, political and economic life. The contestation is that with the change in the ideological and the resultant functionalism of the political firmament at the reigning head, the policies of both external real, and the attendant domesticity, change in nations. New Delhi is no exception to the rule. When PM Nehru commandeered the nation in the aftermath of the Indian independence, then at that point of time, the civilizational idea of an anointed Bharat was relegated to the backburner by the nationalist Congress influenced by the socialist and communist strain of the times. The irony is that the communist cohorts still refrain from accepting the constitutional rule book and the lore of the founding fathers who were their refuge givers and shelter and succour providers.

In the manner in which the political spectrum changed with the rise of stress on inclusivity, social justice and coalition parties, the Indian political firmament witnessed a permanent change with New Delhi becoming g multipolar and very eclectic in its tenor and nature. Prime Minister Narendra Modi and Vajpayeeji ushered in a fresh era of change, systemic revolution both in the domestic realm and in the sphere of foreign policy and foreign affairs. PM Modi too has stuck to the Nehruvian legacy of strategic autonomy of the nation in the realm of foreign transactions but the aggressive, provocative and economic outreach of the New Delhi dispensation has brought a sea change in the identity and the global perch of Bharat. The notion of Cold War politics does not hold itself now in any form and multi-alignment happens to be the order of the day.

Modi has ushered in a new mode of diplomacy inspired by the nom de plume of public diplomacy. The Americanization has taken place at an ideational keel which is a fact which has gone unobserved and unnoticed by scholars and academics of the nation but the West recognizes the transformation in the veneer and tenor of 'New India' with its external and diplomatic ramifications. Regime change and the ideological transformation of the nation have come at a gradual pace which is amply reflected in the foreign policy trajectory in Bharat. The manner in which the de-ideologisation of India's foreign policy has taken place is a phenomenal achievement of the Modi regime. Vestiges of the licence, quota raj still remained in the international trade practices of the land which were being militated against by the Modi dispensation. The statis in foreign policy and diplomacy required a gradual and swift revolution and no better than a Ministry of External Affairs aided by Modi and Jaishankar provided the change and the slow jolt to the sordid saga of sanguinity in the realm of the upkeep and innovation in the sphere of external relations.

Human security is the order of the day in the larger international system. In a world lined by war and aggressive politics, the peace and developmental concerns are hampered and largely obstructed. This paper highlights the negotiation ethics of G20 as a platform of diplomacy wherein the concerns of the South or the developmental needs of the developing nations assume a prominent global concern instead of merely paying lip service to the decisions and monopoly of the First World and the developed comity of nations. This paper highlights the global commons of food security, climate change action, gender empowerment, poverty eradication and conflict resolution which are pertinent requirements of a besieged international system with a Third World tilt, wherein, the hiatus between the on the rise developing world and the first worlders can be emphatically brought out.

India has always been an initiator as far as the notion of human security globally is concerned with special emphasis on the Third World. The religious adherence to the theme of Sustainable Development Goals has been one of the foreign policy fortes of a nation on an upswing. The targets of the order of poverty eradication, women empowerment, labour discourse and others add to the feathers in the cap of the international organizations which New Delhi, too, has been striving for in the larger context of sustainability and returning to Mother Nature in the context of what we have usurped from her. In the earlier United Nations General Assembly gatherings, too, PM Narendra Modi has been raising the voice in the hallowed corridors of international peace and justice. PM Narendra Modi initiated the LiFE initiative in the august presence of United Nations Secretary-General Antonio Guiterres with the objective being to attain a global green scenario.

It has been estimated by experts that even if one billion people out of the global population of eight billion take up the onerous task of adopting a climate friendly and a green lifestyle, there would be a drastic cutback by 20 per cent in the total carbon emissions of the larger international system. The LiFE mission was officially introduced in the Glasgow city's COP 26 in 2021. It was in his words "an international movement towards mindful and deliberate utilization, instead of mindless and destructive consumption" to bring the global system to a greener and much more sustainable future where the Santani perspective of human security goes back to the neophyte times of yesteryears. The National Security Strategy of the United States of America as expostulated by President Joe Biden too mentions India as being the epicentre of liberal democracy and the time is ripe for India to take up a global leadership role along with a regulating role by the USA and other democratic denominations in the larger world.

The G20 Conference of nations was initially defined as primarily an economic grouping. Since the turbulence and transformation in the geo-economics of the globe, a larger and much more eclectic perspective has been adhered to by New Delhi at the crucial Bali conference. Also significant was the Indian insistence on a no-war pact between the global comity of nations other than the impact of the pandemic and the Ukraine conflict and the resultant penury in food and energy supply chains. Despite being an economic construct, it encompasses elements ranging from block chain, global health architecture and emerging technologies to climate change, digital transformation and migration. Equity and inclusion are the other prominent concerns of the Bali Declaration with India assuming the novae leadership in the G20 till 2023.

The Brogen Project informs us that "In many countries, when people hear the phrase 'Third World country', visions of impoverished countries struggling to meet basic human needs are the first to pop up. This might be true in today's society, but the original definition of a Third World country referred to the nations that lacked an alliance with either the USA or the former Soviet Union during the Cold War. In recent years, the term has come to define countries that have high poverty rates, economic instability and lack basic human necessities like access to water, shelter or food for its citizens. These countries are often underdeveloped, and in addition to widespread poverty, they also have high mortality rates."[1] Thus, the disadvantaged sections of countries are placed under the nomenclature of the Third World. The low infant mortality rates along with the scourges of illiteracy, widespread poverty and food security along with malnutrition stand as some indicators of the notion of underachievement in the sphere of human security. Thus, we can conveniently posit the conceptual sect of Third World.

The innovation through the soft power and human security outreach of the nation is a double achievement of the Modi regime. The Nehruvian and its attendant communist mindset though espoused the theme of Third World leadership but India did not have the actual girth and strength of a superpower. The difference now is that Prime Minister Modi is the first stark realist who is preparing India through a transition, both domestically and internationally. First of all he is attempting to attain traction and respect for the Bharatiya capabilities, history, culture, myth and lore which was done in a hodgepodge manner under sub national concerns. PM Modi is removing the Bharatiya guilt and the credo of taking pride in the national heritage and institutional reforms have been propagated and amplified in the larger global realm. The global comity of nations and ecosystem is being made aware of India on the rise of reforms and ease of doing work which can be mutually beneficial to the investor as well as the nation. The great diplomatic amplification which he is striving for is the innovation of not mere borrowing and blandly buying technology and processed from abroad but the comity of developed nations such as EU and the United States of America have been asked to use the technological girth and expertise of Bharat and not mere produce and import from foreign lands and their attendant corporate world.

Modi has realised a few regimental formulations which has transformed the Indian image and a reactive and pacifist and redtapist structure of Bharat. International organizations entail regimes as a core precept of classical but an ever-changing IR theory. John Ruggie writes that "International regimes have been defined as social institutions around which actor expectations converge in a given area of international relations. Accordingly, as is true of any social institution, international regimes limit the discretion of their constituent units to decide and act on issues that fall within the regime's domain. And, as is also true of any social institution, ultimate expression in converging expectations and delimited discretion gives international regimes an inter-subjective quality. To this extent, international regimes are akin to language – we may think of them as part of 'the language of state action.'"[2] The Third World approach can be adapted by the entire world as 'Modi's Approach' which is inclusive about the First World interests too in a non-confrontationist manner of approach with the Occident. Thus, the convergence of the global agenda along with the assimilation of the slower and gradualism of the Third World nations too can embolden and strengthen the strivings to spawn a Third World-friendly agenda globally ranging from climate change concerns to energy and food security concerns. The regime can truly become a regime only if the undeveloped world too assumes a positive and overtly less hostile stake in the development story of the larger international system.

India thus emerges as a true blue and practically effective leader of the Third World as they can actually gain to a certain extent by strengthening Bharat's global oeuvre. Thus, a strong India by 2047 can actually become a global leader in multifarious ways and can done the mantle of a global power in an unhegemonic and non-aggressive manner.

Thus, regime formation becomes the order of the day, wherein, myriad nations and their establishments strive to coalesce into a global whole. India's presidency of the G20 group of nations is a step in the right direction. India has been knocking for long at the gates of the great power status wherein Indian leadership of a new reformed Global South can benchmark the arrival of a new power and the novae Global South, which does not believe in mere protestations against the North and the First World but aims to work as equal partners with the richness and the expediency of a smart group of nations like never before. It is New Delhi that can make the Global South forge a new bridge between the contesting national interests and characters of the northern and southern countries. It can be observed pithily that New Delhi has the potential to envisage a new road and developmental trajectory in the going-ons in the Third World nations and their constituent populations. The larger halo-like approach of engendering a Third World agenda and a novae approach with Indian tutelage can become the nom de plume approach of the developmental agenda of the world.

The Indian and Modi's leadership comes at an interesting cusp wherein the world faces the twin threats of emergence from COVID profligacy and the mayhem and global impact of the Ukraine crisis. It's these twin challenges makes it all the more pertinent for the New Delhi dispensation to forge a bond in the larger international system in order to arrive at the facilitation of the attainment of sustainable goals for times to come. New Delhi can emerge as a crucial instrumentality and a change agent which can take the Global ship out of the sea of a rudderless North-South conflict and forge a conjoined approach onwards a deft geo-economic, geo-political and diplomatic high seat and perch through which conflict resolution and human security can attain a new meaning and deference.

All these developments which are new, novel and innovative shine with the corporate and a professional zeal which the Nehruvian regime disdained to the hilt. The manner in which they took Western help and simultaneously disowned them further exacerbated the global outreach and the global outreach of a nation on the ascendancy and which had a great potential to rise much earlier and be a power to be reckoned with. This was the Nehruvian hitch which the present Delhi dispensation is striving to extricate Bharat out of the entire tandem of affairs in the realm of foreign policy and diplomacy.

The quintessential and traditional IR pet peeve is that the Third World nations and the developing comity of LDCs are pitted against the First World in a zero-sum game since the aftermath of World War II. Nobody can deny the colonial oeuvre of Western domination since antiquity and the history of nations. Still, with the advent of globalization and interdependence, the classic confrontational narrative has changed considerably with the developing world led by nations such as India, China and Brazil adopting a soft approach towards the Western world and specifically, the USA. This was the changed approach of the BRICS groups of nations belonging to a certain comity of interests in the BRICS a few years ago. But the return of international conflict between Ukraine and Russia with NATO's leadership role seems to have deepened the fissures between the developing world and the developed nations of the First World.

In the BRICS 15th summit to be held in South Africa, the stress will be on the de-dollarization of the world economy along with an emphasis on making the global governance system fairer and impartial. The Indian championing of the cause of climate change and SDGs in the broader sense has further added to the strength of the Indian leadership of the developing comity of states along with the fruitful and proactive impact of India's G20 presidency in the current year. The delving into the financial structure of the larger system of geo-economics in the global system is also on the anvil as an agenda theme of BRICS 2023 in South Africa. The *Daily News Egypt* reported that "Among many hopes is that the current BRICS group considers the incorporation of other countries. This will be very important because it will give volume to the BRICS group. Of course, major economies, such those of India, Brazil and China, are there, but if other countries can also be incorporated, the political dimension of BRICS will be improved significantly. So far, over 20 countries have formally applied to become new BRICS members, including Saudi Arabia, Iran, the United Arab Emirates, Argentina, Indonesia, Egypt and Ethiopia."

Thus, the expansion of the BRICS comity of nations and the regional collectivism is another theme which might be discussed and deliberated upon at the Johannesburg Summit. Dissimilar to the theme of the expansion of NATO, the BRICS expansion will only add to the voice and popular acceptance of the BRICS grouping vis-a-vis the developed First World. Along with South-South cooperation, the China-led Belt and Road Initiative is also being praised and diplomatically extolled in the heady and vibrant portals of the BRICS comity of states which might not endear New Delhi with the BRICS agenda through efforts need to be made not to politicise the regional organizations and the credo of regionalism.

Another emergent theme is the participation of the Russian Premier, Vladimir Putin, who has been indicted by the ICC (International Criminal Court). Modi stands firm on the balancing platform and India as a fresh whiff of air sides with no one. This instance of strategic distanciation emerges as another uplifting characteristic of the Modi dispensation in the light of the tricky, treacherous and volatile international system. The reactive and collective approach of the Nehruvian times has now taken a back seat. The popular and legal cacophony is being raised that due to the red marking of Putin, he might be arrested as the ICC has red-inked his name. Some observers are calling the advent of the 2023 Summit as the initiation of the paradigm shift in global geo-politics and geo-economics. With Putin attending the Summit virtually, the deft tightrope walking of several nations with the West and the rest in the light of the Ukraine-Russia war, will be tested and the national establishments will have to further check the strategic and political turf before unveiling a stance on Russia. Also, as an attendant fact, India too finds itself with the same and adroit balancing act which had it posited in the context of the Ukraine-Russia conflagration which is all set to dampen the spirits in the Johannesburg Summit. The Indian stance can get complicated and lead to a complexity of the Johannesburg deliberations. Still, BRICS has to contend with 'bullies' such as Russia and China and how the strategic convergence between the political upstarts in the developing world and the dominance of Russia and China can be balanced, remains to be seen and only time will relate to us the larger geo-political ramifications as they will unfurl before the global comity.

Initially, the term 'BRIC' was introduced to tap the potential of global investors in places such as India, China and Brazil, but since the advent of the pandemic, the Ukraine war, rising awareness of global warming and the dynamic power rivalries amidst the Great Powers, ICS 2023 needs to stick to its larger and broader agenda along with serving as solution provider as the saying goes. BRICS need not be only a congruency platform but must negotiate meaningfully in the larger global firmament.

NOTES

1. Simone Williams. URL https://borgenproject.org/definition-of-a-third-world-country/ (Online Web), accessed on 1 October 2023.
2. John Gerard Ruggie. '*International regimes, transactions, and change: embedded liberalism in the post-war economic order*', Cambridge University Press, 1982.

Index

*